Praise for Dr. Bruce Weinstein's
Life Principles: Feeling Good by Doing Good

"Read this book and re-read it again and again. What a great road map to living and doing well."
— **John McConnell, Senior Vice President of Programming, ABC Radio Networks**

"Dr. Bruce Weinstein's Life Principles *distills a powerful philosophy in a simple and unforgettable handbook for living the ethical life. Indispensable guidelines for a life well lived are a welcome gift in our tenuous times."*
— **Frances Hesselbein, Chairman, Leader to Leader Institute; Former President, Girl Scouts of America; Recipient, Presidential Medal of Freedom**

"Dr. Weinstein's thoughtful book clearly shows that ethical, caring behavior is the basis not only for harmony among people, but also for our own personal well-being. An indispensable book with an important message."
— **Jeffrey Moses, Author, *Oneness: Great Principles Shared by All Religions,* Revised and Expanded Edition**

"Bruce has me convinced: It's not just right *to do right. It's* smart *to do right, too."*
— **Ellis Henican, Columnist, *Newsday*; Political Analyst, Fox News Channel**

"Should be required reading for every level of employee, from the CEO to the sales force and beyond. A must for students in high school, college, and business school, too."
— **Rick Frishman, President, Planned Television Arts; Co-author, *Networking Magic, Guerrilla Publicity*, and *Guerrilla Marketing for Writers***

"In light of the recent wave of scandals throughout America, we seem to have lost our moral compass. Bruce Weinstein's book brings us back to the principles that not only benefit society, but also benefit us professionally and personally. Follow Bruce's advice by taking the high road and you will prosper!"
— **Jordan E. Goodman, author,** *Reading Between the Lies: How to Detect Fraud and Avoid Becoming a Victim of Wall Street's Next Scandal*

"In a time when it seems ethical conduct has gone out of style, Bruce Weinstein provides us an easy road map to doing the right thing."
— **Wendy Zang, Lifestyle Editor, Knight Ridder/Tribune News Service**

"Bruce Weinstein offers readers an insightful and engaging guide on how to navigate life's murky ethical waters in settings as diverse as the office and the neighborhood grocery store. His answer to the age-old question, 'Why be good?' is refreshingly simple and humane."
— **Alison Stateman, Managing Editor,** *PR Tactics*

"Behaving ethically at all times is clearly the right thing to do, but people often assume that ethical behavior comes at a cost, i.e., it prevents one from maximizing wealth. Yet through his Life Principles, Bruce Weinstein explains that ethical behavior leads not only to a more fulfilling life, but to a richer life as well. This is certainly a result all rational human beings would desire."
— **Vahan Janjigian, PhD, CFA, Columnist,** *Forbes Magazine*; **Editor,** *Forbes Special Situation Survey*

"Bruce Weinstein's Life Principles are the Ten Commandments and the golden rule brought up to date and into harmony with the twenty-first century. In this complex age they provide a simple framework for making life meaningful and enjoyable."
— **Jim Ryan, Anchor,** *Good Day New York*, **Fox Television**

"Life Principles: Feeling Good by Doing Good *by Bruce Weinstein, PhD, has taken the discussion of ethical behavior to an inspiring level. A captivating and engaging read based on five ethical principles that can easily be integrated into everyday living, the book is packed with excellent ethical questions to which Dr. Weinstein provides sound answers—along with questions that challenge readers to think about what constitutes 'doing the right thing.' An uplifting read for all ages and all backgrounds!"*
— **Edward Sanders, Editor-in-Chief and CEO,** *Hospitality News*

"Bruce Weinstein shows us how to take the high road to our highest selves. He also reconnects us to the goodness that is at the core of all human beings—a connection we often lose sight of. His message is timely and timeless! This book can make our inner and outer worlds better, richer places."
— **Stacey Tisdale, Financial Journalist; Former Correspondent,** *CBS MarketWatch*

"Dr. Weinstein has written his book with enormous wisdom, insight, and compassion. It should be required reading for everyone to help us all live a better, happier, and more ethical life."
— **Ed Askinazi, Producer, WETA-TV, Washington, DC**

"Dr. Weinstein has a wonderful knack of getting to the flash point of issues we all wrestle with in our lives. Anyone who enjoys a lively debate about our value system should definitely read this book."
— **Tony Haines, President, Digital Video Arts, Jacksonville, Florida**

"Finally there is a guide to ethics in a world that seems to have lost all sense of morality. Dr. Weinstein is truly our nation's conscience."
— **Kevin McCarthy, RPh, Vice President, PharmCon Inc., Continuing Education for Healthcare Professionals**

"*In* Life Principles, *Dr. Bruce Weinstein has laid the groundwork for leading one's life in a commendable, accountable way. I have made changes in my life because of his seminars. I stop and think before I react. I feel better about myself when I do the right thing. I can now lead by example for my children and feel really good about it. Most of the changes are introspective ones, some little, some bigger, but all are positive changes nonetheless.*"
— **Erin E. Halsey, The Scienomics Group, Greenwich, Connecticut**

"*According to Dr. Weinstein's* Life Principles, *physicians are not the only ones who should 'do no harm.' That is just one of five Life Principles laid out by the author that if followed would make us all better human beings.*"
— **Howard A. Heit, MD, Fellow of the American College of Physicians; Fellow of the American Society of Addiction Medicine; Assistant Clinical Professor, Georgetown University**

"*Now, more than ever, we need to take stock of where we are and where we're going.* Life Principles *provides a basic framework for tackling professional and personal challenges, from the biggest to the smallest. It's the ultimate rule book for playing the game of life well.*"
— **William W. Hood III, of Counsel, Isaacson, Rosenbaum, Woods & Levy, P.C., Denver, Colorado**

"*In my line of work, teaching ethics and moral structure to children who have been victimized, and helping them believe that such a structure can be rebuilt in their lives, is the key component to helping them heal and recover. Dr. Weinstein's book will help all of us in making these lessons a reality.*"
— **Diana Goldberg, Esq., Executive Director, Children's Advocacy & Family Resources, Inc./Sungate, Denver, Colorado**

LIFE
Principles

LIFE
Principles

Feeling Good by Doing Good

BRUCE WEINSTEIN, PhD
The Ethics Guy

books

LIFE
Principles

For further information, contact the publisher at

Emmis Books
1700 Madison Road
Cincinnati, OH 45206

www.emmisbooks.com

LIBRARY OF CONGRESS CATALOGING-IN-PUBLICATION DATA
Weinstein, Bruce D.
Life principles : feeling good by doing good / by Bruce Weinstein.
p. cm.
ISBN 1-57860-216-5
1. Ethics.   2. Conduct of life.   3. Happiness.   I. Title.
BJ1581.2.W377 2005
170'.44--dc22

2005003314

Designed by Stephen Sullivan
Edited by Jessica Yerega

PRINTED IN THE UNITED STATES OF AMERICA

For my mom and dad,

who taught me these principles and

showed me why they matter.

DISCLAIMER

Nothing in this book is intended to be legal advice.

Please contact an attorney

if you wish to obtain such information.

CONTENTS

INTRODUCTION

Management is doing things right;
leadership is doing the right things.
—**Peter F. Drucker**

The secret to living a rich, satisfying, happy life is to be found in five simple principles. We've known about these principles for more than five thousand years. Every religious tradition in the world teaches them, as do parents in every country. Without them, civilization would be impossible, because there would be nothing but chaos everywhere. These principles have a transforming effect on who we are and where we go in life. They are the principles of ethics, and they are as follows:

(1) Do no harm
(2) Make things better
(3) Respect others
(4) Be fair
(5) Be loving

Yes, these principles are simple, but deceptively so, because too often we let fear, anger, or other negative emotions get us off track. This creates a downward spiral, and it's sometimes difficult to get back to where we want to be.

For example, how often do we really keep "do no harm" in mind during our daily interactions with people? If a clerk at the grocery store is nasty to us, aren't we tempted to return the nastiness and tell ourselves, "Serves them right"? If we give in to this temptation, we harm the other person. In so doing, we harm our own soul—and that's why we shouldn't return nastiness with more of the same.

In the book you are about to read, we will explore these principles in depth, and we'll see why doing the right thing benefits us in the long run. We'll examine how every religion expresses these principles in one way or another. We'll consider how to apply these principles in our everyday lives. We'll even think about what to do when the principles conflict and seem to pull us in opposite directions.

You might wonder, "If these principles are so commonplace, why should I read a book about them? I already know them. In fact, they're so obvious that reading an entire book about them seems like a waste of time."

It's true that they're commonplace, but it's also true that in our hectic, overcommitted lives, we get so caught up in the details of getting through the day that it's easy to forget how important these principles are in everything we do. We're also tempted every day to place value on things that ultimately aren't that important. So taking a few steps back to consider these principles is a helpful thing to do.

On the face of it, the principles are about making a difference in the lives of other people. To this extent, taking them seriously seems like something we have to do, something we ought to do, something that, quite frankly, we'd rather not do.

What we'll discover in this book, however, is that making ethics our central concern is actually the best way to lead a richer, more fulfilled life. A life that helps us get the things we want: the right partner, a job we love, and a place where we want to live. By taking ethics seriously, we serve as role models for our children and increase the chances that they will go into the world and make us proud.

Recent scandals in the news show the risks we take when we neglect these principles: public humiliation, shame, and in some cases, a prison sentence. But the main reason for taking ethics seriously is not the danger of failing to do so, but rather because it's the right thing to do.

The path to a happier, more fulfilled life lies in becoming reacquainted with the principles of ethics, which tell us how we should treat one another. When we act with integrity, we feel better about ourselves, and we then create the conditions for making many wonderful choices in our own lives.

This, then, is a book about why doing the right thing is the best thing we can do for ourselves. When we take the high road, we give a gift to others—and ourselves. It's the greatest gift of all.

I'll show you why.

FREQUENTLY ASKED QUESTIONS ABOUT ETHICS

Q: *What is the difference between ethics and morality?*

A: Historically there was no difference, because the word from which we get "morality" was the Latin translation of the Greek word from which we get "ethics." If you ask five of your friends to define these terms, you will get five different definitions of each. Both terms broadly refer to "doing the right thing," however, and because one term grew out of the other, we ought to use them synonymously.

The meaningful distinction is not between ethics and morality, but between ethics and the law. That is, something can be ethical but not legal, and vice versa. For example, slavery was legal, but that didn't make it right. Women didn't get the legal right to vote until

1920, but that doesn't mean that in 1919 they had no moral right to vote. When Rosa Parks refused to the move to the back of the bus in Montgomery, Alabama, one afternoon in 1955, she broke the law but did the right thing. Yes, we should take the law into account in our decision making, but for any law we can and should ask, "Is it right? Is it fair? Is it just?" The ultimate standard for deciding how we should conduct ourselves is ethics, not the law.

I don't mean to suggest that we all become anarchists, but rather to acknowledge that laws change, laws vary from state to state, and some laws don't exist that should (hence the saying, "There oughtta be a law…"). Also, the law doesn't apply to some areas of ethics, as we will see later. When we ask ourselves, "What should I do?" what we're really asking is, "What is the right thing to do?" and not merely, "What does the law require of me?"

Q: *What makes something an ethical issue?*

A: Whenever we ask "What should I do?" and our decision is likely to affect the rights or welfare of another person, we are asking an ethical question.

Sometimes when we ask this question, no one else will be affected by what we decide, at least not in a significant way. For example, when we wonder, "Should I wear the red blouse or the blue one? The striped tie or the solid one?" no one else will be adversely affected by the choice we make. It may be a pressing question for us in the morning, but it is not an ethical one.

However, if when we learn that someone at work is using his expense account for personal reasons, or an ATM gives us too much money, or a blind date tells us she wants to see us again but we don't feel the same way, the question "What should I do?" is a matter of ethics. At stake are such responsibilities as maintaining good relationships with colleagues, protecting others from harm, being fair to businesses, avoiding theft, and being true to ourselves. An ethical dilemma arises when we feel a conflict between two or more moral values, and it seems as though we cannot honor all of the values at stake.

It turns out, however, that there are very few genuine ethical dilemmas in the world. It is often possible to find a creative way to fulfill all of the obligations at stake in a sticky situation and to obviate the need for deciding which responsibility, and thus which moral value, is the most important one for us to honor.

One implication of all of this is that we are faced with many more ethical questions than we might otherwise have considered. When ethical issues are discussed in the media, they are often of the life-or-death variety. Abortion, euthanasia, withdrawal of life support, and the death penalty are issues that have not just legal but moral ramifications, and in the public eye they are debated not just by politicians and lawyers but by ethicists and moral theologians. It is a serious mistake, however, to limit ethics to such extreme matters. Confidentiality, truth-telling, and promise-keeping are also ethical issues, even if no one's life hangs in the balance (though that may be the case). In short, ethical issues are at stake in every human relationship and, some would argue, in our relationships with animals and the environment as well.

Ethical issues are everywhere.

Q: *Are there right and wrong answers to ethical questions?*

A: Yes. The following thought experiment will illustrate why this is so.

Suppose you and I are old friends and that we are both psychologists. I call you up one day to ask you for help with an ethical problem I'm facing. "I just started treating a patient who has a lot of problems, and she's going to be in therapy for a long time," I tell you. "But I'm very attracted to her, and I'd like to ask her out on a date. Would that be ethical of me?"

"Of course not!" you respond. "You're a health care professional, and you have a duty to promote your patient's well-being. You'd violate this duty if you crossed your professional boundaries and became intimate with her. Besides, she trusts you to place her needs above your own. Dating a patient is absolutely, unequivocally wrong."

"Well, you have your opinion, and I have mine," I say.

But wait. Wouldn't you agree that any psychologist who believes that it is okay to date a patient doesn't just have a different *opinion* about appropriate conduct? He or she is *mistaken*. In other words, it is wrong to be romantically involved with a patient, regardless of whether a particular psychologist believes otherwise. The ethical rule that psychologists should not become romantically involved with patients is absolute, so if a psychologist were to wonder, "Is it all right to date someone I'm treating?" the answer would be a resounding "no."

This is but one of many examples of an ethical question that has a clear and distinct answer, one that does not vary according to who is asking the question, where he lives, or even what religion he is.

After all, what kind of a world would we have if there were not right and wrong answers to ethical questions? We would have a world that is even more chaotic than the one we have now.

Judgments about food and art are subjective, but not judgments about ethics. Is vanilla ice cream better than chocolate? For you it might be, but not for me. Are Martin Scorsese's films better than Steven Spielberg's? It's a matter of personal preference. However, when we're faced with an ethical problem, it is simply not the case that one response is just as good as another.

Note: I have used the field of psychology merely to make a point. I do not mean to imply that psychologists are more likely to be scoundrels. Every social group has been rocked by scandal, and just about all of us have done things we shouldn't have done.

Q: *Isn't it true that in many, if not most, cases we know what we ought to do, but we don't do it? What gets in the way of doing the right thing?*

A: Fear, guilt, or self-interest. Let's consider these one by one.

Fear: When we see someone doing something he or she shouldn't be doing, especially if it's a co-worker, a student, or a friend, we often decide to do nothing, even though we know it would be better to intervene. We're afraid of damaging our relationship with the wrongdoer, or we worry that he or she will think less of us if we speak our mind. It is difficult, however, to justify actions based on fear, especially when we're in a position to be a force for good and there is no serious threat to us if we choose to act.

Guilt: Physicians, nurses, and other health care providers know all too well that when they are providing care for a patient at the end of life, a family member will often appear out of the blue and demand that everything possible be done to keep the patient alive, even if the patient has signed an advance directive making it clear that he or she wouldn't have wanted such treatment. This evidence is meaningless to a family member who had a falling out with the patient years ago and is now racked with guilt. It is guilt, not a true concern for respecting the patient's wishes, that motivates the demand to "do everything possible" in these situations.

Self-Interest: Sometimes we take the low road simply because we'd rather indulge ourselves than do the right thing. When a clerk accidentally gives us twenty dollars too much in change, we know we should give it back, but if we decide not to, it's because there are things we'd like to buy with the extra cash. As the rash of business scandals has shown us, however, unethical conduct can come back to haunt us. It may be easier to take the low road, but in the long run it's simply not prudent to do so. Of course, the main reason we should do the right thing is that it is the right thing to do, but if it helps to consider the personal benefits too, so be it.

Q: *In calling yourself "The Ethics Guy," are you implying that you're always ethical or that you're better than the rest of us?*

A: Not at all. I would never suggest that I always do the right thing, or that I am morally superior to anyone. This question reminds me of how a practitioner of meditation and martial arts responded when someone said to him, "It must be wonderful to be centered all the time."

"I'm not always centered," he replied. "It's just that when I'm off-center, I know that I am, and I know how to get back."

Similarly, my work in ethics has sensitized me to the ethical issues that exist in my relationships. When I make a mistake, which I do all the time, I'm aware of the problem, and I do my best to correct it. Of course, it's one thing to know that one has erred, and it's another thing to have the courage to make amends. Like everyone else, I know I can do a better job of doing the right thing, and I pray for the compassion of others when I don't act appropriately.

Q: *Ethics, schmethics. Wouldn't the world be a better place if everyone simply followed the golden rule?*

A: Not necessarily. Consider the following scenario: Imagine that you are a surgeon who is performing surgery to save someone's life, and the patient begins losing blood rapidly. If you do not give her a blood transfusion immediately, the patient will die. Should you give her the blood?

"Absolutely," you might say. "I have a duty to save her life."

But suppose also that you are a Jehovah's Witness, and you believe that it is sinful to accept blood or blood products. If you take the golden rule, "Do unto others as you would have them do unto you," as your guide, you would say, "Because I wouldn't want the transfusion if I were in the patient's situation, I will not give it to her either." But that can't be the right course of action, because it would impose your idiosyncratic values and beliefs on your patient.

We can preserve the well-intentioned spirit behind the golden rule, however, by tweaking it slightly: "Do unto to others as they would have you do unto them." This way, you can operate (literally and figuratively) under your value system and at the same time honor your patient's values, which may very well be different from yours. Of course, you are not obligated to do anything the patient wants simply because he or she asks you to do so. This version of the golden rule simply recognizes that physician and patient may come together with different values, and this difference does not present insurmountable obstacles to working with one another.

Even the smallest towns in America are home to a wide range of religious and moral communities: Christian, Jewish, Muslim, Buddhist, Hindu, atheist.

When we come together for business or personal reasons, the new version of the golden rule allows us to be true to our own traditions while respecting the values of others, which may be different from ours.

The old version of the golden rule worked well in homogeneous communities (like, for example, Mayberry, where everyone but Otis pretty much had the same values). In the twenty-first century, however, it is time to recognize the limits of this rule and to forge a new guideline so that we may live and work together peaceably and with dignity.

WHAT'S YOUR ETHICS IQ?

Circle the option you would choose in each scenario, then add up the point values assigned to each of your choices. After learning about the five Life Principles, you will find an analysis of each option in the section titled "Your Ethics IQ Revisited" at the end of the book.

What would you do?

1. After leaving a grocery store, you notice a six-pack of soda sitting in an otherwise empty shopping cart in the parking lot. Would you:

   A) Leave the soda where it is.

   B) Take it and keep it.

   C) Bring it back to the store.

2. A friend recently set you up on a blind date, which didn't go well. Your friend, who is extremely sensitive to criticism, asks you how it went. Would you:

A) Lie and say it went well.

B) Tell the truth.

C) Thank your friend for the set-up but be vague in your answer ("Well, we'll have to see; you never know about these things...").

3. You are at a party and one of your friends has become intoxicated. As she prepares to leave the party and drive home, you tell her that she has had too much to drink and that you will take her home. She rudely tells you to mind your own business. Would you:

A) Do as she says.

B) Take her keys away from her and arrange for a way for her to get home.

C) Call the police when she gets on the road and tell them that an inebriated person is on the loose.

4. You have just opened your own retail pharmacy. One of your competitors sells cigarettes, which bothers you, because you feel that health care professionals should do what they can to prevent harm to others. On the other hand, cigarette sales

are lucrative, and it is getting harder and harder to make a decent living these days. Would you:

A) Refuse to sell cigarettes.

B) Sell cigarettes but caution customers about the health risks of smoking.

C) Sell cigarettes but without the lecture.

5. Your friend asks you if you like the new dress she has just purchased. You think it looks horrible but don't want to hurt her feelings. Would you:

A) Tell her the truth.

B) Find something about the dress that you do like and mention only that (e.g. "Rayon is so easy to care for!").

C) Use language that is accurate but deceptive ("It's incredible! I've never seen anything like it!").

6. You see an expensive article of clothing that you want but can't afford. Would you:

A) Save your money and buy it later.

B) Buy it now, wear it once, and then return it.

C) Sign up for the store's credit card or use one you have and get it now.

7. You and your beloved are having dinner at a fancy restaurant to celebrate your anniversary. When the check arrives, you notice that the waiter forgot to include the expensive bottle of wine you had. Would you:

A) Pay the bill without notifying the waiter of the omission but leave a larger tip than you had planned.

B) Pay the bill as is and leave a normal tip.

C) Tell the waiter about the error.

8. One evening while watching TV you discover that you are now receiving a premium cable channel that you have not ordered. After doing some research, you learn that the cable company has made a mistake; it is unwittingly providing the service without charging you for it. Would you:

A) Do nothing but enjoy the free service.

B) Contact the cable company and notify it of the error.

C) Wait a few weeks to see if you really watch

the channel that often; if not, call the cable
company and have it removed.

9. While you are driving on the highway, a driver
passes you and cuts you off as you're preparing
to change lanes. You are startled and scared by
his actions. Your children are in the back seat.
Would you:

A) Roll down your window and yell at the driver.

B) Call the police on your cell phone while
you're driving to notify them of the incident.

C) Stay calm and do what is necessary to protect
yourself and your kids.

10. A celebrity, once one of your favorites, was
recently convicted of a serious offense and
sentenced to prison. How do you feel about this?

A) Glad that the person got what s/he deserved.

B) Sad that someone you used to admire gave in
to less-than-noble impulses.

C) Numb.

Determining Your Ethics IQ

Note the point values assigned to the choices you made in the "What would you do?" quiz, add them up, and then find your score below.

Question				Score
1.	A=2	B=1	C=3	_____
2.	A=1	B=3	C=2	_____
3.	A=1	B=3	C=2	_____
4.	A=3	B=2	C=1	_____
5.	A=1	B=3	C=2	_____
6.	A=3	B=1	C=2	_____
7.	A=2	B=1	C=3	_____
8.	A=1	B=3	C=2	_____
9.	A=1	B=2	C=3	_____
10.	A=1	B=3	C=2	_____
			Total	_____

If you scored...

10–15

You demonstrate a tendency to take the easy path, which is not necessarily the best path. Ethics is about taking the interests of others at least as seriously as we take our own interests, but a score in this range suggests a preference for your own needs and wants. Ironically, in the long run you are likely to thwart your own goals by acting selfishly. We'll see in the discussion that follows that taking the high road isn't just the right thing to do; it is beneficial for us. The reason to be ethical isn't personal gain, but this is a nice side effect.

16–25

Sometimes you choose to do the right thing, and sometimes you don't. It's understandable that you occasionally lack the courage to take the high road—no one is perfect—but ethics demands consistency of behavior when the circumstances warrant. It is not okay to be a saint at work and a sinner at home. If we aspire to be the best person we can be, it is in our own interests, as we shall see, to strive for doing the right thing in all of our interactions with people.

26–30

You are to be commended for taking the high road time and time again, even when it would be easier in the short run to do otherwise. Whether you make the right choices because you were raised to act responsibly, or because you have learned through experience that everyone wins when we do the right thing, or because of some other reason, you are a virtuous person. May others be fortunate enough to learn from the example you set.

You are probably wondering now, "Who is to say which choices in the scenarios are the best ones?" Or, as some of the folks in my hometown of Brooklyn might ask of me, "Who died and made you boss?" The scores for each response are not based on my own values or personal preferences but rather on the five Life Principles that we will now discuss. After we have examined the principles and seen how they apply to specific circumstances, we'll revisit the quiz and see how the Life Principles show us which choices are the best ones.

To paraphrase Bette Davis from *All About Eve*, "Fasten your seat belts. It's going to be a thrilling ride!"

LIFE PRINCIPLE #1
DO NO HARM

Will you try to change things, use the power that you have,
the power of a million new ideas?
—Robert Lamm, "Dialogue (Part I)"

Just as a house needs a strong foundation so that it can do it what was meant to do, society needs a strong moral foundation to function effectively. The most fundamental building block of any society is Life Principle #1: Do No Harm. This principle is both the most important of the five Life Principles and the easiest to put into action. It is the most important because we would live in constant fear if we could not trust others to take the principle seriously (either because they want to or because they know that there are severe consequences, like prison, if they don't), and it is the easiest because, in most cases, all we have to do is…nothing.

Let's explore Life Principle #1 more closely and see why it is in our own interest to take it seriously.

Defining Harm

Harm is damage to the function, appearance, or feelings of another, or to its goals or interests. In one sense it is an objective concept. Parents understand that the medicine they take can make their children sick, so good parents use childproof containers and keep the vials away from their children's easy reach. Cat lovers know that certain houseplants are dangerous to their pets, so they avoid having those plants around, no matter how pleasant they may be. Similarly, no one has to be convinced that, all things being equal, getting shot or stabbed is something to be avoided. Most of us value having healthy children, pets, and bodies.

It is when we look closer at the concept of harm that problems start to appear. Is it harmful to lose a job that one depends on for sustenance? Yes, at first blush, but getting fired can lead to better things, so in the long run, and with the benefit of hindsight, it can be a good thing. (For real-life examples of this, read Harvey Mackay's book *We Got Fired! And It's the Best Thing that Ever Happened to Us.*) Does giving someone a friendly pat on the back harm them? Not in most cases, but if the person happens to be recovering from back surgery we may unwittingly cause pain or even injury. Are frightening movies harmful? For the squeamish and highly sensitive they might be, but horror fans not only are immune to strong images; they thrive on them.

The lessons from these observations are threefold: 1) What appears harmful can turn out to be helpful, 2) Good intentions don't always produce good consequences, and 3) There is a subjective component to the concept of harm. By "subjective," I mean that for us to understand whether something is helpful or harmful to another person, we have to know something about his or her values, preferences, and psychological make-up—in short, what kind of person he or she is.

For inanimate objects like furniture or stereo equipment, values and preferences don't play a role in questions of harm. If you drop the book your friend loaned you in the toilet, ruining the delicate illustrations it contains, you've harmed the book—and perhaps your friendship—simply because you've made its function of being pleasing to the eye harder to obtain. When your toddler pours orange juice in your cable

TV box, he has made it more difficult to get clear (if any) reception. Things are harmed when we make it harder for them to do what they are meant to do. But sometimes to know whether our actions harm another human being, we have to know first what that person considers important, valuable, or pleasing.

Basic Goods, Essential Values

From the above observations, one might conclude that because it is hard, if not impossible, to know fully the values and preferences of every person with whom we come into contact or have a relationship, we can never know if our actions are likely to cause harm. This is simply untrue, because at the most basic level of our existence, we want the same things:

- ❖ To be free from pain and discomfort
- ❖ To be treated with respect
- ❖ To love and be loved
- ❖ To have enough to eat
- ❖ To have clothes to wear
- ❖ To have a safe place to live

Not included on this list are those things we may want but don't truly need: a U2 iPod, a white BMW convertible, or an all-expenses-paid trip to the Hotel du Cap in the south of France. These are nice to have but are not of fundamental importance (unless your film has been accepted to the Cannes Film Festival and the Hotel du Cap is the only place left for you to stay).

In other words, we can reasonably foresee which actions could harm someone else, because others have the same basic needs and desires that we do. You don't need to know anything about the people on the street to see that the extra-large umbrella you are toting around could poke them in the eye, which they would surely consider harmful. It doesn't take a PhD in clinical psychology to know that a flip remark about someone's weight gain could hurt her feelings. A sober person knows that a drunk person behind the wheel spells trouble for all concerned. Fulfilling the "do no harm" principle here means, above all else, being aware of the people around us. Getting outside of ourselves. And then being willing to take a few simple steps to prevent injury, hurt feelings, or untimely death—the ultimate harm.

Do No Harm in the Real World

It is impossible to apply Life Principle #1 completely and in every circumstance. A nurse causes pain to a child by giving the child a flu shot, thereby harming him (causing him discomfort) in the short run, but that nurse also prevents harm in the long run by inoculating the child against a potentially life-threatening illness. The nurse could harm the child more by withholding the shot; yes, the child would be spared pain for the time being, but he would be at risk for more pain and worse through this choice. In effect, the nurse and the child's parents perform a moral calculus: On balance, it is less harmful in the long run to give a flu shot than to withhold it.

In practical terms, Life Principle #1 has three formulations:

(1) Do no harm
(2) Minimize harm
(3) Prevent harm

Let's next consider how we might apply these three rules in our daily interactions with people. Along the way we'll see why taking them seriously isn't just the right thing to do; it's good for us in the long run.

Applying Life Principle #1 in Everyday Life
SHOULD I GO TO WORK WHEN I'M SICK?

Q: *Is it wrong for me to go to work when I have a cold? I don't like the idea of infecting other people, but my job places a lot of demands on me, and if I stay home for even a day, the workload when I return is overwhelming.*

I figure that if I take the proper precautions, like covering my mouth when I sneeze and washing my hands frequently, I can greatly reduce the risk of infecting other people. What do you say?

A: It is unethical for you to go to work when you are sick for two reasons: 1) you have an obligation to others not to make them sick, and 2) you have an obligation to yourself to get better. You cannot fulfill either of these duties if you go to work with a cold. Practicing good personal hygiene can reduce but not eliminate the threat to others, and being in a stressful environment like the workplace makes it more difficult to recover from even a minor illness. This is in part a management issue; a good boss would not allow workers to come to work sick, in part because she has a duty to protect workers from harm, but also because sick workers cannot do their jobs effectively.

It is noble of you to take your job so seriously that you would give more importance to your work than to your personal comfort, but there is no shame in tending to your own needs. In fact, in this case, it would be wrong to deny yourself the pleasure of a day at home with a mug of tea and your favorite TV show. Just remember the golden rule (which, contrary to how many people act these days, is not, "Do unto others *before* they do unto you"). It's quite possible that you got a cold because someone else came to work sick. Why not take the high road and give yourself—and your coworkers—a break?

HOW SHOULD I END MY RELATIONSHIP?

Q: *I recently became intimate with a man I'd been dating for about a month. We met through an online matchmaking service and clicked, so to speak, right away. However, I have decided that I really don't have room in my life right now for a serious relationship, because I am very busy pursing my career goals. Since we began our relationship through e-mail, I feel that it would be okay to break it off the same way. Am I wrong?*

A: Yes, you are. If the relationship had progressed no further than e-mail exchanges, or perhaps if you'd had a single date and then decided he wasn't for you, an e-mail Dear John letter would be fitting. By stating that you "became intimate," however, you indicate that you have had a deeper level of involvement, which ethically requires a more personal level of communication. You haven't indicated whether you have developed any kind of feelings for this person, but it may very well be the case that he has developed feelings for you, and he would almost certainly be hurt by being let go via the Internet. Yes, some of the hurt feelings would be a result of the relationship ending, but part of it would likely be the manner in which you revealed your decision to him. The right thing to do would be to call him and tell him how you feel, or perhaps even to arrange to meet him briefly in a public place and let him know face-to-face.

Your question may strike some as simply a matter of etiquette, not ethics. However, whenever we ask, "What should I do?" and the decision we make could harm another person, then we are faced with an ethical question. Ending a relationship almost always hurts at least one of the people involved, and that hurt can be quite painful. In the world of dating and romance, it is not possible to avoid causing harm, but we can and should minimize the harm that can come from breaking up.

WHAT SHOULD I DO IF I THINK I WITNESSED ADULTERY?

Q: *Last night at a bar I spotted my best friend's husband passionately embracing another woman. Although I was troubled by what I saw, I decided to mind my own business. Was that wrong of me?*

A: Yes. It's important to pay attention to the little voice that tells you something is amiss. Of course, the first step to making a good decision is to get the facts, and you don't know what exactly was going on. It would have been perfectly reasonable to call the man aside and tell him what you observed. If it turns out that he really was being unfaithful to your friend, simply calling him on it could very well make him rethink his actions. Some might argue that you should even tell your friend what you saw. That, however, would probably cause undue alarm, and she might take her anger out on you. It's possible to protect both your friend and yourself.

SHOULD I HAVE CONFRONTED AN ABUSIVE STRANGER?

Q: *The other day I saw a woman yelling at and slapping a young boy who was with her at the grocery store. The child couldn't have been more than four or five and apparently had taken some cereal off of the shelf and put it in the shopping cart. The mother's behavior was abusive, but I didn't say anything because I felt it was none of my business. My husband says I should have spoken up. Who's right?*

A: Your husband is. All of us have a moral duty to prevent harm to others if we're in a position to help and if, in so doing, we're not placing ourselves in great danger. For example, if you were an excellent swimmer and noticed someone drowning in a pool that had no lifeguard on duty, you would have an ethical (but not necessarily a legal) obligation to get into the water and try to save the person's life. That wouldn't be the case if you couldn't swim and would risk drowning yourself. (You could still help by calling for assistance, though.) Likewise, it would take very little effort to say something to the woman like, "I know that our kids sometimes get the best of us, but perhaps there are better ways of correcting their behavior, no?" If she told you to get lost (or worse), it would be time to get the manager of the store involved. Extreme cases of child abuse ought to be reported to child protective services.

People like this woman who act abusively in public and who are not confronted are given license to continue with their harmful behavior. By speaking up, you may not be thanked for being a caring person, but that woman will almost certainly think twice before losing her temper again.

We have a moral obligation to look out for one another. That is what being a member of a community—and being human—means. If you don't stand up for that child, who will?

HOW SHOULD I DEAL WITH A ONE-NIGHT STAND?

Q: *Last Saturday night I met a cute guy at a bar, and after a few too many drinks, we had unprotected sex at my place later that evening. The next day he told me that he had a girlfriend, so I threw him out of my apartment. My best friend is now on my case for two things: for sleeping with someone I hardly knew, and for not telling him that I have herpes. My feeling is that this creep deserves what he gets. What do you think?*

A: Your position is totally irresponsible. First, you had unprotected sex in an era where AIDS poses a significant threat. Second, you suggest that two wrongs make a right. (They never have, and they never will.) It is one thing to *feel* justified in keeping potentially harmful information from your one-night stand. It is quite another thing to *be* justified. It is understandable that you would be hurt and angry by being misled, but you do no one any good by withholding the fact that you have a sexually transmitted (and transmissible) disease. How would you feel if this man now unwittingly gives herpes to his girlfriend? Why does she deserve your wrath? Or suppose they have a child together, and the infant gets the virus. How do you justify that?

You can take the high road, put your feelings aside, and prevent further harm to people, or you can take the low road and live spitefully. The choice is yours— and I hope you'll make the choice that I'm sure you know in your heart of hearts is the right one.

You also might consider whether it is in anyone's interest, including yours, to have unprotected sex with a stranger again.

WHEN IS IT TOO LATE TO RIGHT A WRONG?

Q: *I work in a fast-food restaurant, and three months ago, my coworker (let's call him John) spit on a hamburger patty that was intended for his math teacher who had given him a D on his last test. I thought it was funny at the time, but my girlfriend told me that this guy could have infected the teacher. Is it too late to do anything about the incident, or should I just forget it?*

A: It is never too late to right a wrong. You should tell John that you've been thinking about the incident and, even though you laughed when he did it, you've had second thoughts. Your girlfriend is right; John could indeed have made his teacher sick. Even if that never came to pass, however, what John did was disgusting and completely inappropriate. If this coworker threatens to pull a stunt like that again, tell him it's not funny and that you'll tell the manager if he doesn't cut it out. You could even tell John that if he really wanted to get back at his teacher, he should ace the next test.

For the record: A teacher doesn't "give" a student an A or a D; the student earns it.

SHOULD I IGNORE OFFENSIVE HUMOR AT WORK?

Q: *My coworkers frequently make jokes that I think are in poor taste. In fact, these remarks sometimes make me feel uncomfortable, because they're often of a sexual nature, and sometimes they're just flat-out racist. I don't like to be a stick in the mud, but from my point of view, we're here to get a job done. Do you think I should tell the boss, or just try to focus on my work and ignore what I hear?*

A: Your coworkers have no right to engage in this kind of behavior. First, these jokes offend you, and understandably so. Second, if clients overheard such nonsense, they would rightly consider taking their business elsewhere. You are in a position to prevent harm to your company's reputation. Third, the head of the organization would be livid to discover that such shenanigans were taking place in his or her place of business. For these reasons, you have a moral obligation to do something rather than nothing. Tell the boss.

SHOULD I TELL MY KIDS NOT TO TAKE DRUGS IF I USED TO?

Q: *I want to talk with my preteen son about the dangers of using drugs, but I'm afraid that he'll consider me a hypocrite since I used to smoke pot as a teenager. The fact is that pot is much stronger now than it was in the early '70s, and besides, just because I used to smoke it doesn't mean that he should. Is this a case of "Do as I say, not as I do?"*

A: Not at all. You are not a hypocrite; you are a good parent. We all do things in our youth about which we are not particularly proud. Even if it weren't the case that marijuana is more potent today than it was thirty years ago, you not only have a right to apprise your child about the dangers of taking drugs; you have a duty to do so. The first obligation of parents is to protect their children from harm, and smoking pot is not a healthful practice for young people.

Even if one argues that adults ought to be free to take drugs in the privacy of their own homes, it doesn't follow that children ought to have such freedom. We don't let children drive. We don't let children use firearms. And we shouldn't sanction children smoking pot.

Be honest. Let your son know how much you care about him. Tell him not only *that* he shouldn't take drugs, but *why* he shouldn't. I hope you will find the courage to have this important conversation with your son—soon.

LIFE PRINCIPLE #2
MAKE THINGS BETTER

Turn the darkness into light
Turn the hunger into life
Turn the wrong into right
Put an end to the strife
—Steve Miller, "I Want to Make the World Turn Around"

It would be an empty life indeed if our only guide were Life Principle #1: Do No Harm. Suppose you're a physician and after a hard day on the job you come home and your husband or wife says to you, "How was work today, honey?"

And you say, "It was great. I didn't kill anyone or make them worse off in any way!"

The good physician does more than avoid harming patients. He makes them better. Doctors in particular, and health care providers in general, have as their mission the restoration of health. That's what they do.

But the idea of benefiting others shouldn't be limited to doctors, nurses, pharmacists, dentists, and other health care professionals. All of us would do well to live by Life Principle #2: Make Things Better.

Strictly speaking, this principle is not as strong as Life Principle #1. That is, it is more important to avoid harming people than it is to help them. Although it is easier to apply Life Principle #1 than #2, since Do No Harm requires either avoiding action or taking only minimal action, it is a mistake to rank these principles. Both are part of a checklist we should consider when deciding how to act.

One of the main differences, though, between Life Principles #1 and #2 is that Do No Harm applies to everyone who could be affected by our actions, while #2 has to, of necessity, be applied selectively. Even Mother Teresa could not possibly benefit everyone in the world, though she went further than most of us in getting there.

Before we consider to whom we should apply Life Principle #2, let's unpack the notion of benefit.

Defining the Notion of Benefit

"Benefit" comes from the Latin root "bene," which means "good." When we benefit someone or something else, we contribute toward its flourishing. Watering a plant gives it the elements it needs to grow, just as feeding a child does. Benefit is a continuum concept:

The most basic goods	**Luxury items**
Necessary for survival	*Pleasing but not necessary*

The further left we go on the continuum, the more objective the notion of benefit becomes. At the far left, few would dispute that food, clothing, shelter, and health are basic needs. Without any of these, survival would be impossible. At the far right lie those things that we might like but can do without. But depending on our values, how we were raised, and what our expectations are, we might feel we need things that others would consider nice to have, perhaps, but not essential. An investment banker living in a five-bedroom apartment on Park Avenue may feel he needs such accommodations to maintain his social standing and self-esteem; those who do not move in such circles may look upon such a lifestyle as extravagant.

Beyond the most basic goods that all of us agree are necessary for survival, there is not a consensus about what constitutes a benefit. That which you consider good is based upon your values and preferences, and these may differ greatly from mine. For example, if you love to cook, watching the Food Network, trading recipes with friends, and perusing catalogs of the latest cookware is beneficial to you. If your idea of cooking, however, is throwing a plastic bowl of Easy Mac into the microwave, you would consider these activities to be a waste of time.

Nevertheless, in our effort to apply Life Principle #2 in our everyday life, it is helpful to consider the various ways in which we might benefit others.

Benefiting Ourselves and Others

Human beings have the following dimensions:
- ❖ Physical
- ❖ Psychological
- ❖ Spiritual
- ❖ Relational

There are not sharp distinctions between these categories. In spite of Rene Descartes's claim the mind and body are two separate entities, we now know that the two have a close relationship to one another. Our attitudes and beliefs can affect our physical health, just as physical illness can affect our mental health.

Benefits to others in each of these categories include, but are not limited to, the following:

Physical:
- ❖ Providing food, clothing, and shelter
- ❖ Assisting with mobility or transportation
- ❖ Promoting the functioning of the senses
- ❖ Alleviating physical ailments

Psychological:
- ❖ Alleviating or managing obstacles to our mental health, including anxiety, depression, obsessive-compulsive disorder, and addictions (These disorders also have physiological components, though.)
- ❖ Promoting self-confidence and self-esteem (Although we cannot "give" someone these qualities, we can do things that contribute toward their development and maintenance.)

Spiritual:
- ❖ Enriching the soul (For many, this means developing or improving one's relationship with the Deity.)

Relational:
- ❖ Promoting strong relationships with family, friends, and coworkers
- ❖ Creating and sustaining intimacy with a partner

Giving Yourself to Those Who Matter Most

There is only so much of ourselves we can give without becoming spiritually, emotionally, and financially bankrupt. How should we decide who has a rightful claim on the goods we can bestow upon them?

All things being equal, the closer someone is to us, the stronger our duties are toward him or her. Consider Diagram A on the following page.

It's unfortunate to miss a friend's birthday, but it is unconscionable to forget your spouse's. It is kind to listen compassionately to a coworker's complaints about her deadbeat husband over lunch, but it is obligatory to alleviate your children's anxiety about going to school for the first time.

The following diagram is only a guideline for rank-ordering who in our lives deserves our help. Through their actions, people can move closer or further away from us, and even blood relatives can fall out of our graces permanently:

Everyone else
Fellow citizens
Members of the immediate community
Boss, coworkers, assistants
Oldest and best friends
Distant family
Immediate family
Spouse or partner
Self

Diagram A

Fredo, you're nothing to me now. You're not a brother, you're not a friend. I don't want to know you or what you do. I don't want to see you at the hotels. I don't want you near my house. When you see our mother, I want to know a day in advance, so I won't be there. You understand.

—Michael Corleone in *The Godfather, Part II*, after learning that his brother Fredo played a role in an attempt on Michael's life

Of course, Michael's ultimate response to being betrayed by his brother—authorizing Fredo's murder—was extreme, and it revealed how much Michael had deteriorated morally. As we will see in our discussion of Life Principle #4, the punishment has to fit the crime.

Applying Life Principle #2 in Everyday Life

WHAT SOCIAL RESPONSIBILITIES COME WITH NETWORKING?

Q: *Each month I hold networking parties for members of my business community. Earlier this year I introduced two people—let's call them Jane and Joe—who have mutual commercial interests. I never heard from either of them after the party. Last week I received an angry call from Jane, who told me, "How dare you not tell me Joe was married? You have no right to be running network-ing meetings." It turns out that Jane and Joe started dat-ing shortly after the networking party, and the relationship had become quite intense. I told Jane that I never had any intention of making a love connection; my introduction was strictly for business purposes. Did I do the wrong thing?*

A: Jane is, understandably, quite upset about being duped, but she is taking her anger out on you, and that's wrong. You are a networker, not a matchmaker, so any adult who enters into a romantic relationship as a consequence of these parties is going above and beyond what you're offering. Of course, Joe should be ashamed for misleading Jane, but that's his burden, not yours. Some people will blame you for their own poor judgment or the misfortunes that befall them, but that's not your problem.

You can tell Jane that you are very sorry for what happened, but you should also stand up for yourself, since Jane is treating you unfairly. If it turns out that Joe is a predator and is using your meetings to do his dirty work, that would justify kicking him out. For now, stay out of Jane and Joe's romantic troubles, and don't flag from your well-intentioned efforts to promote business in your town. There is only so much one person can—or should—do.

WHEN IS IT TIME TO END A FEUD?

Q: *Earlier this year I loaned a friend a valuable book he had admired, and he returned it in worse condition. The pages are now dog-eared, and some have greasy fingerprints on them. Upon receiving the book in such shape I was livid, and I told him so. He told me that he took great care with the book and was offended that I would suggest otherwise. We haven't spoken since. Since it is now the holiday season, I would like to let bygones be bygones, but I don't know what to say, since I still feel he treated my belongings (and thus me) with disrespect. What do you advise?*

A: Your first mistake was loaning something valuable to a friend. "Neither a borrower nor a lender be," said Polonius to his son in Shakespeare's *Hamlet*, and this advice from four hundred years ago still makes good sense. Since you've already committed the error, however, you have to move forward and make the best of the situation.

What it comes down to is this: What is worth more to you, the book or the friendship? I suspect the latter is the case, since you feel bad that the relationship took a turn for the worse, even if, from your point of view, you did nothing wrong. It is quite likely that your friend feels the same way. I suggest that you make a peace offering in whatever way you see fit; ask him to go to a movie or make plans to have lunch, and then put the matter behind you.

Next time, either don't loan things at all or be prepared to get things back with some wear and tear. Expect others to treat your belongings less gingerly than you do, and you'll never be disappointed.

IS IT WRONG TO RE-GIFT?

Q: *Last year I got a sweater from a friend—let's call her Joy—for Christmas. The sweater was very unappealing to me, and I could never imagine wearing it. I value my friendship with Joy, however, and didn't want to hurt her feelings, so I thanked her for the gift. I then gave it to another friend of mine, Sally (not her real name), who had seen the sweater in my closet and admired it. But wouldn't you know, Joy called me last night and said she saw someone else wearing the sweater around town and was deeply hurt that I had given it away. Did I do the wrong thing? How should I patch things up with Joy?*

A: It is not unethical to "re-gift," provided that:

(1) You make sure you don't re-gift to the original giver.
(2) You don't use the gift first.
(3) The new recipient doesn't know the original giver and/or is not likely to run into him or her (if the gift is an article of clothing).

If someone else might enjoy or be able to use a gift we don't want or need, we not only have a right to give it away; we have an obligation to do so. After all, it is wasteful not to put something to good use if we can.

All is not lost, however. If you explain to Joy why you gave Sally the sweater and let Joy know that you really do value her friendship, you may very well be able to minimize whatever hurt she feels now. In the event that Joy is so livid that her anger continues to burn brightly and she won't accept your apology, it might be worth reconsidering the value of the friendship.

WHAT IS THE PROPER FAST-FOOD ETIQUETTE?

Q: *Do I have an ethical obligation to clean up after myself at fast-food restaurants?*

A: Strictly speaking, no, you do not. Cleaning the dining area is the role of restaurant employees. However, although you would not be doing wrong by getting up and leaving your tray, food wrappers, and empty cup for the eatery's staff to dispose of, Life Principle #2 invites you to go the extra mile and dispose of your refuse yourself. After all, it takes little effort to do so, and the next person to sit where you did will appreciate having a clean table on which to eat. Besides, the clean surface you enjoyed may very well have been the result of a previous customer acting on this Life Principle. Particularly during peak business hours, fast-food places may not have enough staff to bus tables fast enough. "That's a management issue," you might say. "It's not my problem." Technically, you're right, but with all of the effort you expend in deciding whether you have a duty to clean up after yourself, you could have just as easily tossed your garbage and been on your way.

Besides, cleaning up after oneself is a good habit to get into. Take the high road, leave your environment as clean or cleaner than you found it, and you'll both benefit others and feel good about yourself—without so much as breaking a sweat.

SHOULD I FORGIVE MY BROTHER?

Q: *Years ago my brother and I had a falling out. He made a pass at my wife, and I have never forgiven him.*

He has reached out to me several times, but I have rebuffed his efforts. Oddly enough, my wife has put the incident past her, but I find myself unable to do so. Do you think that there are certain things a person can do that justify writing him off for good?

A: Perhaps, but this occasion isn't one of them. People make mistakes, and people can also redeem themselves. There is no excuse for what your brother did, but by turning away his good-faith attempts to renew his relationship with you, you are also engaging in wrongful conduct. Life Principle #2, Make Things Better, calls upon you to move forward with your sibling. First, you have to find some way in your heart to forgive him. It might be helpful to discuss with a therapist, clergyperson, or other trusted advisor what is preventing you from doing so. Then, and only then, will you be in a position to reestablish a connection that is both meaningful and likely to withstand future challenges.

What would the world be like if it were not possible to right our wrongs? Not one I'd want to live in—and I'll bet that's the case with you, too.

LIFE PRINCIPLE #3
RESPECT OTHERS

R-E-S-P-E-C-T
Find out what it means to me
—Otis Redding, "Respect"

Imagine someone who cared nothing about your privacy, who routinely broke promises to you, who lied on a regular basis, and who blabbed your most delicate secrets to anyone and everyone. No matter what interests you might have in common with this person, there is no way you could ever consider her a worthwhile friend. In fact, if you look back on your life at the relationships you decided to end, you'll probably find that the common denominator in most—or even all—of them was the failure of the other person to respect you. Respect is an essential moral principle in every relationship we have: with our friends, with our family, with our coworkers, and even with total strangers.

In some ways, the moral principle of respect for others is a new idea in civilization. After all, cultures with a history of slavery didn't apply this principle uniformly. In the United States, women didn't have the legal right to vote until 1920. And informed consent is a relatively recent development in health care. Nevertheless, at least some elements of the broad notion of respect, such as the duties to be honest and to keep one's promises, are to be found in every culture and religious tradition around the world.

Even today we can find examples within each culture and religious tradition of practices that violate the principle of respect for others, but this reflects a failure of human beings rather than any limitations of the principle itself. No one can argue with the importance of respect; the problem is that we as fallible human beings often find it difficult to apply this principle in our professional and personal lives.

The responsibility to respect others is based on the idea that every person has certain rights, not in virtue of what he has done, but in virtue of who he is: a human being with intrinsic worth. If someone has a right, then others have a duty toward her. Your right to be treated with respect means that others have an obligation to treat you with respect. Some rights flow from the kind of relationship two people have. If you are my patient, for example, I have a duty to obtain an informed consent from you before I provide treatment, so that you have the necessary information to decide whether to accept or reject various treatment options. (For more on this topic, read Ruth R. Faden and Tom L. Beauchamp's *A History and Theory of Informed Consent.*)

The principle of respect for others is the basis of several specific moral responsibilities. Whether the social context is home, work, or the community, we should:

- ❖ Tell the truth.
- ❖ Keep our promises.
- ❖ Respect privacy and keep confidences.

These are not necessarily legal obligations. If you promise a friend that you'll meet her for a drink after work but something better comes along and you lie to your friend to get out of the commitment, you have violated two of the above duties, but you haven't broken any law. Besides the absurdity of having a government be that intrusive, it is hard to imagine how a law prohibiting the breaking of promises could be enforced.

When you call your friend and say, "Esmeralda, can we take a rain check on drinks today? My boss suddenly dumped a project on me that has to be completed this evening," when the truth is that another friend, Enrique, can get you on the guest list with him to a hot new dance club, you don't have to worry about being arrested for fibbing to Esmeralda.

That doesn't get us off you off the hook, though. By taking the easy way out, you have let Esmeralda down, even if she doesn't know it (yet). More to the point, though, you have let yourself down, because you have put a dent in the trust that your friend placed in you. You may get something you value in the immediate future, but you lose some of your integrity in the process. If you do this often enough, you may find that there isn't much left to lose.

The Three Elements of Respect for Others

It is one thing to say that, in theory, we ought to respect others, but how do we put this idea into practice? What are some useful ways to resist the temptation to take the easy way out? How should we respond when we're faced with a choice between doing the right thing, which we might not want to do, and doing the thing that appears to be more pleasing, satisfying, or gratifying in the short term? Let's consider these questions with respect to three elements of Life Principle #3.

TELLING THE TRUTH

The obligation to be truthful is one of the most fundamental duties we have to one another. No relationship could exist for long if we didn't have faith that what the other person tells us is, to the best of his knowledge, true. The saying "Honor among thieves" implies that even when a group is made up of crooks, that group depends upon truthfulness within itself to be able to function.

If you are a physician, for example, and you've just diagnosed cancer in a patient who has a lot of anxiety about the symptoms she's been experiencing, how should you respond when she asks you, "I don't have cancer, do I?" As frightening as the diagnosis of cancer is, the principle of respect for others demands that you be truthful. Lying to the patient to protect her from harm actually harms her in another way: It shows contempt for her.

Of course, being truthful doesn't mean being brutally honest. One can and should temper one's duty to tell the truth with other duties that we'll discuss later in this book, such as the duty to be compassionate. But the bottom line is that when we owe someone the truth, we do a serious injustice to them—and to ourselves—if we withhold it.

The duty to tell the truth applies to every realm of human experience, including the political realm. One of the lessons we've learned from former Presidents Richard Nixon and Bill Clinton, as well as other politicians who have become ensnared in their own lies, is that Americans have a great capacity for forgiveness. What we have little tolerance for is deceit.

Many people argue, in fact, that Clinton's greatest sin was not having an extramarital affair but lying about it. Suppose that, instead of wagging his finger condescendingly to the press and emphatically stating, "I did not have sex with that woman, Miss Lewinsky," he simply admitted that he'd made a mistake. It might have been shocking, and perhaps in the short run his popularity would have dipped, but in time the event would have become old news. But as we know, that's not what happened. Instead, he held his ground, and for far too long the country was immersed in this sordid tale.

Being honest in particular, and respectful of others in general, is a very powerful way of being an ethical person. Why should we care about this? Because being ethical, doing the right thing, and acting from principle rather than from fear are among the most noble things we can do. When we do these things on a regular basis, especially when we do them sincerely, from the heart, and not out of guilt, we create a life of wealth and abundance. A life of riches in the things that matter most. And unlike stocks, bonds, and cash, these riches can never be taken from us.

We end the day being able to look ourselves in the mirror, sleep peacefully, and awake with the knowledge that by taking the high road, we have benefited not just others, but ourselves.

PROMISE-KEEPING

Let's consider again our earlier example of Esmeralda and Enrique. You've just made plans to have dinner with a friend of yours, one you haven't seen in a while. On the day of the occasion, another friend calls you and invites you to a party you'd really love to attend, but to do so, you'd have to break the engagement with your first friend. You'd rather go to the party, but you've already promised your friend you'd spend time with him. What should you do?

One of the rules that keep relationships in working order is the rule of keeping our promises. After all, our word would be meaningless if we broke it on a regular basis. At the heart of this moral obligation is the concept of trust: We maintain the trust that people place in us by, among other things, keeping our promises.

There are always extenuating circumstances that justify breaking a rule. If, for example, your parent is rushed to the emergency room an hour before your dinner date, you not only have a right to reschedule the dinner, but you have a moral obligation to do so. Your duty to your parent outweighs your duty to your friend. The example of the conflicting social invitations, however, doesn't involve a life-or-death decision. It presents the all-too-common dilemma of being confronted with a more tempting option than the one for which we've already made plans.

Let's assume for the sake of argument that you can't bring your first friend to the party, for whatever reason. It would not only be rude to break off the dinner date, it would be unethical, because it would involve breaking a promise simply to indulge your own desires. By keeping the date, you maintain your integrity, and you'll feel better about yourself, even if you end up sacrificing what seems to be the more appealing opportunity. And who knows? You may end up enjoying the dinner after all.

The concept of fidelity, or loyalty, is closely related to promise-keeping. From the Latin root "fide" we get not only "fidelity" but "confidentiality" (as well as "Fido," the standard nickname for dogs, the most faithful of pets). When we speak of a professional having a fiduciary responsibility to a client, what we mean is that the professional has an ethical obligation to be loyal to his client. This duty is tied to the very notion of professionalism. In fact, the word "professional" comes from another Latin word, which means "to make a public declaration." The professional publicly declares to devote his knowledge or skills to the benefit of others. This does not mean that physicians or attorneys have to be self-sacrificing. Rather, professionalism means that in choosing to become a doctor or lawyer, one's primary mission is not to enrich oneself. We go to our physician or lawyer rightly expecting that the recommendations we get will be based on our best interests, not theirs. We trust them to do what is right for us, since they have pledged to do so.

Professionals aren't the only ones who have a duty to keep promises, however; all of us do. Sometimes we create that duty ourselves, such as when we declare, "I promise to call you." Sometimes the duty is created for us, such as when we are hired to do a job. Signing a contract for employment is a legal act, but it is also a form of promise-making and is therefore an ethical act as well. We pledge to our employer that we will do the job that is asked of us. Our employer, in return, promises to create a work environment that allows us to do our job and, every two weeks or so, to pay us. If we routinely spend our time at work surfing the Internet for shopping bargains or yakking on the phone with friends, we've not only violated our contract; we've broken our promise to our employer and are no longer entitled to remain an employee in good standing. Similarly, if we do our job well but our employer fails to pay us or turns a blind eye to reports of sexual or racial harassment in the workplace, the company has broken its promise to us, and we are entitled to redress. (Whether it is in our best interest to file a lawsuit is another matter.)

Adultery is one of the most egregious violations of our duty to keep promises. The fact that it is as common as it is does not lessen the pain that it causes. It destroys trust, sometimes permanently, and forever alters the way the betrayed views the betrayer. From a psychological perspective, adultery is a complex phenomenon. If you love your spouse but have an affair or a one-night stand, you might wonder what motivated you to do such a damaging thing to your beloved. You might spend time with a therapist trying to discover the unconscious motivations for doing something that you know is harmful and is in no one's long-term interests. It may take months or years to uncover the cause behind this destructive act, or you may never even find out why.

From an ethical perspective, however, adultery is easy to analyze. It is wrong, because it violates the duty to keep one's promises and thus treats one's beloved with the utmost disrespect. It is the quintessential violation of Life Principle #3. To notice in one's pattern of relationships a tendency to have affairs with men or women who are married suggests fertile soil to be tilled with a psychotherapist, but it is not an issue that one has to wrestle with ethically. Of course, it is one thing to know that something is wrong and another thing to have the courage to turn away from it. The point here is that sleeping with someone who is not your girlfriend or boyfriend, husband or wife, life partner or significant other, betrays the trust he or she has been placed in you. What is a wedding vow if not at its core a moral pledge to be loyal to one's husband or wife? When we have even what seems like a harmless fling, we break the promise we made before the people we care the most about.

Now that we know the "why" of keeping promises, here are some simple ways we can apply this aspect of Life Principle #3 in our business and personal relationships:

(1) Don't make promises you can't keep.

(2) Keep the promises you make.

(3) If you can't keep a promise for a legitimate reason (which does not necessarily include something better coming along), be honest with the person to whom you made the pledge.

CONFIDENTIALITY

Consider the following situations:

* You go to a therapist for help in resolving a sexual problem you're having.

* A friend tells you that she is getting divorced and asks you to keep this information between the two of you.

* You talk with your rabbi, priest, or minister after your spouse tells you he's been having an affair.

* You sign an agreement at work pledging not to

discuss office matters with people outside the company.

In each of these circumstances, something private is shared with another, and its revelation to third parties could be hurtful, embarrassing, or shameful. The ethical rule of confidentiality is both an attempt to prevent these bad consequences from happening and an attempt to realize the principle of respect for others.

When we uphold confidentiality, we maintain the trust others place in us, and we therefore feel better about ourselves.

Why Respecting Others Is Also Good for Us

The reason why we should tell the truth, keep our promises, and respect the privacy of others is because other people have a right to be treated this way. A pleasant consequence of so acting is that we feel better about ourselves. When I began giving lectures on ethics after receiving my PhD in 1989, I thought that I could appeal to people's moral sensibilities in discussing various ethical problems of the day. Surely an analysis of the principle of respect for others, complete with a history of this philosophical concept, would win the day. What I learned, however, is that most of us—myself included—have a different agenda when we're presented with what we ought to do. In the back of our minds, we ask a simple question, and until this question is answered, we are not fully receptive to the message. The question we ask is this: "What's in it for me?"

This question is rooted in human nature, and nothing that philosophers, behavioral scientists, or our mothers will ever do can change the fundamental need for personal gratification.

The good news is that all roads lead to nirvana (the place, not the band, though perhaps that too). When a tempting alternative comes up at the end of the day after we've made a commitment to a friend, it really doesn't matter if we do the right thing because God, Immanuel Kant, or the voices of our mothers say we should, or because we'll feel better about ourselves if we take the high road. Psychologists like Jean Piaget and Lawrence Kohlberg say that we have fully developed as moral human beings when we see beyond ourselves and consider how our actions will affect other people, but from an ethical perspective, does it matter what motivates you to do the right thing as long as you do it? Ideally, yes; practically, perhaps not.

If you're still not convinced that you'll be better off

by taking the high road, consider how you'll feel if you blow your friend off with a lie, then you run into her by accident later that night. You'll have to make up yet another lie to cover your tracks, and unless you're a very practiced liar (which raises moral questions of its own), the redness of your face and other forms of non-verbal communication will give you away.

Each one of us benefits by taking the principle of respect for others seriously. By honoring our responsibilities to tell the truth, keep our promises, maintain confidentiality, and remain trustworthy, we give a gift to all of those with whom we have a relationship. By enriching others, we enrich ourselves.

Applying Life Principle #3 in Everyday Life

HOW SHOULD I HANDLE CONFLICTING JOB OFFERS?

Q: *I am a recent graduate from college and have been looking for a job for the past four months. Finally there has been some activity, and two companies have shown interest in me. As I interviewed with one company this past Thursday, they offered me a job. I immediately accepted out of desperation and excitement at the offer. However, a company with which I had a series of interviews offered me a job the next day. I am now torn between the two companies, the latter being my first choice but the former being the company to which I made a commitment. Would it be unethical to change my mind and decline the first company's offer and accept the second one?*

A: It would not be unethical to change your mind, but it would be wrong to get out of your commitment to the first company by telling a lie. It would also be wrong to withhold from the second company the fact that you have already made a commitment. The right thing to do would be to have an open and honest conversation with both firms. You might begin with Company #2 and say something like, "I would love to accept your offer, but another company offered me a job, and I accepted it. However, I would like to let the other firm know about your offer and see if they would be willing to let me take yours. Would that be all right with you?" You should be just as transparent with the first company.

If you take this approach, several things are likely to happen: The interviewers at Company #2 will see that you are a person of integrity, and they will think even more highly of you than they already do. They will probably take you on, provided that you are able to get out of your previous commitment. Upon learning of your change of heart, the employers at Company #1 will doubtless be disappointed, but they will understand.

This is yet another example of why taking the high road is not just the right thing to do; it's the path that is most likely to benefit you in the long run. After all, by speaking candidly with both companies, you'll start your career with the knowledge that you acted honorably, and that is bound to strengthen your self-esteem.

SHOULD I GIVE IN TO MY BOYFRIEND?

Q: *My boyfriend has been pressuring me into having sex. He says that if I really love him, I would show him how much he means to me. I do love him, but I'm not ready to have sex yet (I'm fourteen). He's going to college in the fall (he's eighteen), and I'm afraid that if I don't go along with what he wants then I'll lose him. I can't go to my parents, because they don't like him and have told me I can't see him, but they don't know him like I do. What should I do?*

A: Your boyfriend is not only deeply disrespectful of you, he is a potential criminal. You probably don't want to hear this, but your parents are absolutely right in wanting you not to see him. A four-year age difference is insignificant between forty-something adults, but it is a gap the size of the Grand Canyon when the two parties are a freshman and a senior in high school.

True love is based on mutual respect. If your boyfriend really loved you, he would respect your decision to refrain from having sex. Life Principle #3, Respect Others, is fundamental in any relationship; without it, there is no possibility of having anything lasting and meaningful. Another consideration is Life Principle #1, Do No Harm. Simply put, a fourteen-year-old isn't equipped to handle the emotional challenges that come with being sexual, and the threat of sexually transmitted diseases and pregnancy is real and significant.

It will be hard for you to see this now, but getting rid of this guy is the best thing you could do for yourself. Stick to your guns and don't take any nonsense from anyone.

HOW CAN I GET MY MOTHER TO RESPECT OUR DIFFERENCES?

Q: *Every time I get together with my mother, who is a devout Christian, she likes to regale me with modern-day miracles that have been occurring on missionary trips to remote locations in China, Africa, and other places. The problem is, these miracles seem a little too far-fetched (i.e., a tree aging about one hundred years overnight), and the only evidence of these happenings is word of mouth.*

Whenever I confront my mother that this information has no basis in fact, she becomes hostile and defensive and accuses me of not believing in God, which is not the case. How can I present a reasonable argument to my mother without offending her? Whatever approach I take seems to be dismissed by her as being cynical and atheistic.

A: Your question reminds me of a Henny Youngman joke. A guy goes to a doctor and says, "It hurts when I move my arm like this." The doctor replies, "Then stop moving your arm like that!"

Wouldn't it be best for you and your mom to avoid certain hot-button topics altogether? It would be a mistake for you to present a "reasonable argument" designed to take issue with your mother's beliefs, just as it is a mistake for her to tell you stories that you have told her upset you. Why not say to her, in a loving way, "Mom, I respect your beliefs, even if I don't agree with them, and I ask that you do the same for mine." The situation you describe presents the potential for damage to your relationship if both of you fail to honor Life Principle #3. Isn't your relationship with your mother more valuable than being right?

SHOULD I READ MY DAUGHTER'S DIARY?

Q: *My teenage daughter is running with the wrong crowd, and neither my husband nor I can understand why. She comes from a good home, and we've always done our best to instill a sense of right and wrong in her. I know that she keeps a diary, and I'm tempted to read it when she's not here in hopes of finding clues to her behavior. Would this be the right thing to do?*

A: No, it wouldn't. Your impulse to protect your daughter is honorable. After all, a parent's first obligation to her child is to ensure the child's safety. Breaching her right to privacy isn't the way to go about this, though. She will rightly experience this as a profound violation, and this will make your relationship even more difficult than it already is. The good news here is that it is possible to respect her right to keep her personal thoughts private and to help keep her on the right path. The way to do this is to have an open and honest discussion with her about your concerns, and then to do something that all of us find very difficult: listen nonjudgmentally. That means taking to heart what she says, not interrupting her, and reaffirming your love for her. Let her know that you have faith that she will do the right thing. You can always discipline her if she continues her troublesome behavior—just do so short of delving into her personal effects.

DID I DO THE WRONG THING AFTER MY BLIND DATE?

Q: *I recently had a blind date with a woman, and although the evening was pleasant enough, I didn't really feel a "spark." However, I thought it would be nice to develop a friendship with her, so I wrote her an e-mail and said as much. She replied that it was "unethical" of me to e-mail her and would have preferred a phone call. This took me aback, since I know a lot of guys in my position wouldn't have even contacted her at all. I thought I was doing the right thing. What do you think?*

A: Unless you led her to believe that you were attracted to her and wanted to see her again, it was not unethical of you to write her rather than call. Perhaps a phone call would have been more personal, but given the facts of the situation, such an action falls into the "above and beyond the call of duty" category (no pun intended), rather than the "ethically required" one.

In a scenario discussed earlier in this book, I suggested that a woman who had become intimate (her word) with a man would be acting unethically in ending the relationship with an e-mail, since her level of involvement implies a greater degree of commitment and thus requires a more direct and personal response. In your case, however, there isn't a reasonable expectation of continued contact, so not only did you have no ethical duty to call her, it would not have been wrong if you had not even sent her a polite e-mail.

Her accusation of unethical conduct is probably hurt masquerading as self-righteousness. No one likes to be rejected, but it would have been more honest on her part to acknowledge the rejection rather than to take out her upset feelings on you.

SHOULD I BE HONEST IF IT MEANS HURTING MY FRIEND'S FEELINGS?

Q: *A friend of mine asked me if I liked her new dress. I was surprised by her choice because it made her look heavier than she is, and my friend is very sensitive about her weight. Fortunately, her cell phone rang just as I was about to speak up, and when she finished her conversation, we got onto a different topic. I'm afraid, though, that the question will come up again. What's the right way to respond?*

A: Two Life Principles are at stake here: Do No Harm, and Respect Others. You seem to have a dilemma, because taking Do No Harm seriously would point you in the direction of not telling her what you think of the dress, but Respect Others seems to point you in the direction of telling her. After all, she asked you for your honest response, and it would be disrespectful to lie to her.

Or would it? If she truly wants to know your take on her outfit, then telling her a lie violates your duty to treat her respectfully. How likely is it, though, that she wants the truth? After all, she has already bought the dress. It's one thing if you're both in a clothing store trying on various outfits and she asks for your opinion before she makes the purchase. It's another thing if she has already decided it's for her. What she probably wants is not the truth but what Oprah might call "validation." She wants to feel good about her purchase—and by extension, herself—so telling her your true feelings gives her exactly what she *doesn't* want.

You can honor both the Do No Harm principle and the Respect Others principle by finding something flattering to say about the outfit that is sincere. Surely there is something that appeals to you about the dress, so why not say something like, "I've always liked you in bright colors," or, "That would go so well with your favorite purse." In the unlikely event that she presses you for more, then you will have to decide whether it is more important to avoid hurting her feelings or to tell her the truth. In that case, if she really wants the truth, then she ought to be willing to accept it, whatever that may be.

LIFE PRINCIPLE #4
BE FAIR

I was brought up to cheat
So long as the referee wasn't looking
—**Mick Jagger and Keith Richards, "Winning Ugly"**

I don't tip because society says I gotta. I tip when somebody
deserves a tip. When somebody really puts forth effort,
they deserve a little something extra. But this tipping
automatically, that's…for the birds. As far as I'm concerned,
they're just doin' their job.

—**Mr. Pink, from Quentin Tarantino's *Reservoir Dogs***

The character depicted in the Rolling Stones song knows he is being unfair but blames his behavior on his upbringing. Mr. Pink, on the other hand, believes his position is a just one. In his view, what is unfair is the expectation that customers tip their servers. Unlike Mick and Keith's creation, Tarantino's finds fault with society for the injustice at hand.

Like many of us, both characters look everywhere but within in attempting to make sense of various wrongs in the world. What is fairness? Why is it so important? How can taking fairness seriously enrich our own lives? These questions will be the focus of this chapter, and we will see that it makes good sense that treating one another fairly should be a Life Principle.

The Threefold Concept of Fairness

We can learn everything we need to know about the concept of fairness by looking at how some children behave at birthday parties.

Imagine you have a son, Larry, for whom you throw a birthday party one Saturday afternoon. Your sister brings her two boys, Curly and Moe, to the celebration. (Naming one's children after members of the Three Stooges is an ethical issue worth addressing elsewhere!) When Moe gets a bigger piece of birthday cake, Curly feels it isn't deserved. "That's not fair," Curly cries. The boy might never have complained had he been given the same sized slice if he were alone, but seeing someone who appears no different from him get a bigger piece strikes Curly as wrong, unjust, unfair. If there is a good reason to give Curly a smaller piece (say, for example, he is overweight), it is justifiable to cut different sized pieces of birthday cake for the two boys. In fact, it is not only fair to do so; it would be wrong to do otherwise, since one boy deserves a smaller piece (hence the term "desert," or that which is deserved). Parents who feel they are being fair by giving two boys with different needs the same amount of dessert are not giving them their just deserts.

Now suppose that your sister explains to Curly why he is getting a smaller piece, but this reason does not placate the lad, and he throws a temper tantrum. "All right, young man, now you won't get any!" your sister tells him. "I'm taking you home, where you won't get any cake. And because you're acting so childishly, you won't be allowed to watch TV for the rest of the weekend."

This response, of course, makes Curly even more upset, and your sister has to carry the despondent child out to her car, since his yelling and screaming are throwing a wet blanket on the party.

Curly's tantrum is now justified, however, since he has been on the receiving end of a true injustice: Banishing him from the party and taking away his television privileges for so long seems, by any reasonable standard, an excessive punishment. It is, in short, unfair. You feel so bad about the turn of events on Larry's special day that you decide to make up for the interruption by having your spouse run out to get the latest child-friendly video game that all the kids will enjoy.

This thought experiment introduces us to three branches of the concept of fairness:

(1) Distributive justice, which refers to how scarce resources are made available to a group of people with varying needs, desires, and other factors;

(2) Retributive justice, which refers to how we punish those who violate standards of behavior; and

(3) Rectificatory justice, which refers to how we rectify a situation in which a person or group of persons has been treated unfairly.

Let's examine each in turn.

DISTRIBUTIVE JUSTICE

"You can't always get what you want," sang Mick in another Rolling Stones song, but he was wrong in concluding that "if you try sometime, you just might find you get what you need." All you have to do is turn on the news, pick up the paper, or reflect on your own life to see how off the mark Sir Mick was. There isn't enough of anything to go around, and it is hard to find anyone who feels they're fine with what they have. Since we live in a world of scarcity, it is natural to want to know how we are to divide what there is among those who want or need it. In their book *Principles of Biomedical Ethics*, Tom L. Beauchamp and James F. Childress identify the following as standards we might use to make such a decision:

(1) To each person an equal share
(2) To each person according to need
(3) To each person according to effort
(4) To each person according to contribution
(5) To each person according to merit
(6) To each person according to free-market exchange

One standard is not necessarily better than another, as Beauchamp and Childress note. Context is everything. For a birthday party in which some children are on a restricted diet because of their weight, it would be wrong to employ Standard #1, "To each person an equal share," since what is fit for one child would be unfit for another. It would be just as wrong to use Standard #5, "To each person according to merit," because children have equal merit when it comes to getting cake (as opposed to advancing in a spelling bee or musical contest). In the context of a party, Standard #2, "To each person according to need," seems like a better criterion to use in distributing goods like cake and ice cream.

When the resources are organs for transplantation, however, Standard #2 is controversial. Some argue, for example, that lifestyle choices that adversely affect one's health—deciding to smoke or failing to seek treatment for alcoholism, for example—should play a role in determining who is to be given a transplant when there are not enough organs to go around. Obviously this is a complex issue and is beyond the scope of this book to address adequately. (One interesting article on the subject is "Should Alcoholics Compete Equally for Liver Transplantation?" written by Alvin H. Moss and Mark Siegler and published in the March 13, 1991, *Journal of the American Medical Association.*) The point is simply that when we have to decide who gets what, no one standard applies to every situation. "One size fits all" might apply to baseball hats or mood rings, but it certainly doesn't apply to how we realize the Life Principle of fairness.

RETRIBUTIVE JUSTICE

Deciding who gets what of a limited amount of goods or services is one aspect of fairness. Judging whether someone should be punished—and, if so, in what way—is another. This second dimension of fairness is retributive justice.

Whether the question is how to punish an employee who has violated company policy or to what extent we should "lower the boom," as they say in Texas, on a misbehaving child, a good manager or parent takes seriously the duty to be fair. What standard or standards might we use in deciding whether to punish someone at all and, if so, in what way? The simplest answer to this complex question is this: The punishment should fit the crime. Deciding whether or not a proposed punishment is fitting requires a thorough accounting of the facts, an understanding of the relevant law (if the infraction involves a breach of civil or criminal law), and a commitment to disregarding everything about the situation that is not relevant to the matter at hand.

When a person accused of wrongdoing is punished in a way that seems unfair to him, that person is likely to claim discrimination. But is discrimination necessarily unfair? No, it isn't.

Universities legitimately discriminate against students whose grade point averages and SAT scores are below a certain level. Employers discriminate against applicants who lack the requisite knowledge or skill sets, and that's perfectly acceptable. Single people discriminate against suitors to whom they aren't attracted or with whom they do not share fundamental values, and rightly so. To discriminate is simply to make a judgment based on certain standards or criteria. A student's GPA is a legitimate basis for a college to use to separate suitable candidates from those who belong elsewhere. Discrimination is unfair only when it is based on criteria that are irrelevant to the decision at hand.

What constitutes irrelevant criteria? The answer is, again, context-dependent. The standards that are acceptable in one area amount to prejudice in another. It is wrong to use the ability to play Scrabble well as a factor in determining who is entitled to rent an apartment, but if you want to compete in Scrabble tournaments, that skill is and should be the primary, if not sole, determinant of acceptance.

Title VII of the 1964 Civil Rights Act prohibits basing employment decisions on such factors as race, religion, gender, veteran status, and age. Each of these personal characteristics, however, may be a legitimate basis for screening some people in and others out of a group beyond the workplace. Is it wrong to exclude non-Catholics from a Catholics singles mixer? It is hard to see why. If you never served in the armed forces, could you reasonably be denied membership in the local Veterans of Foreign Wars club? Of course. If a personal quality is relevant to the position to which someone aspires, it is acceptable to use that quality as the basis of discrimination. If a quality is irrelevant, it is wrong to use it.

In grappling with what kind of punishment is fitting for a child who misbehaves, an employee who breaches company policy, or a student who cheats on an exam, we must exclude all those considerations that should not play a role in our decision making. The following questions are right to consider in our efforts to come up with a fair response to these challenging situations:

- ❖ What was the nature of the offense?
- ❖ How many times has the person committed the offense before?
- ❖ What is the magnitude of the harm that resulted from the infraction?
- ❖ Were the consequences of the offense reasonably foreseeable?

If the misconduct occurred in an institution, is there a policy that specifies what the punishment is to be? If so, is it fair?

If the misconduct involves a violation of the law, what does the law specify as a punishment? If so, is it fair? (Granted, the latter question applies only to those in the judicial system, but the judges entrusted with the responsibility of applying the law should still take the notion of fairness into account.)

On the other hand, the following people are all guilty of using irrelevant criteria in meting out justice:

❖ The college president who responds to a student's violation of the honor code with merely a stern warning because that student's parents donate a lot of money to the school

❖ The CEO who responds to an employee's harassment of a coworker with indifference "because the guy is a friend of mine"

❖ The parent who turns a blind eye to a child's pot smoking "because it would be hypocritical of me to punish him for something I did myself as a teen"

Situations like these result in unfair outcomes—and the failure to honor Life Principle #4.

RECTIFICATORY JUSTICE

The term "rectificatory justice" is just a fancy way of saying, "Making things right again." When a person or group of people has been the victim of injustice, he, she, or they are entitled to some sort of compensation. This might involve money, goods or services, or simply an apology. In Kirby Dick's powerful documentary *Twist of Faith*, Tony Comes, the film's protagonist and a rape survivor, has what he believes is an achievable goal: He wants the Archdiocese of Toledo to apologize for the sexual assaults that one of its priests, Father Dennis Gray, committed years ago. What happens at the end of Tony's journey provides one of the most chilling and disconcerting conclusions to a film, non-fiction or otherwise, that you're likely to see.

While retributive justice is concerned with responding fairly to the perpetrator of wrongdoing, rectificatory justice focuses on how the good parent, employer, or society should care for the victim of another's wrongful conduct. As is the case with distributive and retributive justice, our efforts to "make things right again" do not flow from a rigid formula or set-in-stone criteria. Rather, one seeks to combine knowledge of the facts with an application of the relevant moral rules, along with the wisdom that can come only from experience.

Applying Life Principle #4 in Everyday Life

SHOULD I TELL ON A CLASSMATE FOR CHEATING?

Q: *I'm in the eighth grade, and the other day I saw a guy in my class copying from the girl next to him during a test. He knows I saw him, and he begged me not to tell the teacher. He promised not to do it again. I went along with it. Did I do the right thing?*

A: No, you didn't. A person who cheats during a test demonstrates that he isn't completely trustworthy; you can't be sure that he won't cheat again. By taking what isn't his—stealing, in other words—he is cheating the entire class. You owe it to this person, to your classmates, and to yourself to tell the teacher what you witnessed. No one likes to be a snitch, but the alternative is worse, since the problem will continue. By taking action, you have a great opportunity to be a force for good. If you keep the matter to yourself, no one wins in the long run. The choice is yours.

SHOULD I REPAY MY FORMER CREDITORS?

Q: *Seven years ago I filed for bankruptcy when my small business went under. I owed seven different businesses* *and people around $120,000. Since that unfortunate experience, my new business has done quite well, so my wife thinks I have a duty to repay my former creditors. I say that because I no longer have a legal obligation to pay them back, I'm in the clear. With whom do you agree?*

A: Your wife. Your situation highlights the difference between a legal obligation and a moral one. Just because the law no longer obliges you to repay your debts doesn't mean you have no moral duty to do so. Morality holds us to a higher standard than the law does. If, for example, you promised your wife you'd take her out for brunch on Sunday, but at the last minute you decided you'd rather watch a football game, you've committed no crime, but you've acted wrongly (assuming she feels let down by your sudden change of heart). It isn't illegal to break a promise for selfish reasons, but it's wrong.

Put the law aside for a moment and think about the folks who provided their goods and services to you. They did so fully expecting to be paid, as you would have in their position. In effect, you made a promise to them, so failing to repay your debt when you're in a position to do so represents a failure to keep your promise. If it is hard for you to see beyond yourself and your own needs, consider how you may be permanently destroying the trust that others have placed in you if you don't repay your debts now that you can. Restoring your social standing isn't the main reason to pay back what you owe, but it is a happy consequence of doing so. Those businesses may not want to work with you again (can you blame them?), but they will think well of you if you go above what the law requires and show that you are a man of honor by taking Life Principle #4 seriously.

IS THE CUSTOMER REALLY ALWAYS RIGHT?

Q: *I manage a small restaurant in a city where there are few "mom-and-pop" operations left. My team and I take pride in going the extra mile for our patrons, but something happened recently that bothers me. A customer ate most of her meal and then complained that it was not properly prepared and "didn't taste quite right." She requested not to be charged, or to be charged only half the menu price. I didn't want to lose her as a customer, so I didn't charge her. Did I do the right thing?*

A: No. It is admirable that you are committed to customer satisfaction, but this woman was trying to take advantage of you. Surely she knew after one or two bites that the meal wasn't to her liking, so that would have been the time to complain. Certainly your server checked in on her at some point, and if she didn't let her know that something was amiss, waiting until the meal was almost over wasn't the time to bring up her concerns. Just as we can err by not giving enough, we can also err by giving too much of ourselves. Both tendencies violate Life Principle #4. You missed a golden opportunity to challenge this customer's beliefs about the rules of dining out, so she may very well feel entitled to repeat her behavior at your restaurant or elsewhere.

If you find yourself in such a situation again—and you surely will—why not say something like, "Ma'am, your satisfaction is very important to me, but if I gave a free meal to everyone who finished most of their dinner, I would quickly be out of business, and that wouldn't do anyone any good." A rational person will respect this response. Anyone else is someone you don't want as a repeat customer.

Your customers have rights, but you do, too. Stand up for yourself, and you will be treated with the respect you deserve.

IS IT FAIR TO OPEN MY BUSINESS TO EVERYONE?

Q: *I own a coffee shop in a part of town where there aren't any public restrooms. Although I have a sign that says clearly, "Restrooms are for customers only," I know that people who don't patronize the business come in, use the facilities, and then leave. I have such a small, busy staff that it's hard to enforce the policy, but sometimes I wonder if I should be more vigilant about doing so. What's your take on this?*

A: As a small business owner, you do not have an ethical obligation to assist the public with their daily ablutions. Creating and maintaining public restrooms is the mandate of city planners, not café owners. However, it isn't wrong for you to allow the public to make use of your facilities. It is above and beyond the call of duty to do so. Your generosity may eventually lead to new business, but even if it doesn't you should be praised for your compassion.

Up to a point, that is. Your first obligation is to ensure that the needs of your customers are met, and if the traffic from the non-paying population interferes with this (for example, by making it harder for the "legit" folks to go to the restroom, or by leaving the facilities in an untidy state), then you not only have a right to draw the line, you have an obligation to do so.

ARE FIXED GRATUITIES FAIR?

Q: *I manage a small office, and I decided to take the staff of eleven out to a nice dinner to celebrate the holidays. When we were given our menus, I noticed a small statement at the bottom: "A gratuity of 25 percent will be added to groups of six or more." What? I think it's unfair to require parties to tip at such a high rate, but more to the point, the restaurant should have told me about this rule when I made the reservation. I didn't want to make the bill an issue during our celebratory time, so I expressed my concern afterward in a letter to the manager. She wrote back and said that because the wait staff has to work extra hard for large parties, she felt the 25 percent rate was justified. This restaurant happens to be one of the best in town, so I really don't want to stop going there, but this experience left a bad taste in my mouth, so to speak. What do you think of all this?*

A: A restaurant can charge whatever gratuity it wants to for large parties, as long as it apprises patrons of the policy when their reservations are made. After all, we are free not to give the establishment our business if we think the rate is too high. But it is not only wrong for a restaurant to spring the surprise on customers at the point of service; it is bad for business. You will probably think twice before making a reservation there again—who could blame you?—so in the long run the restaurant may have lost a valued customer. You might have considered bringing up the matter before you ordered, but then the losing party would have been the server, who was expecting a 25 percent tip.

In her letter to you (a phone call would have been better, if you had provided a number), the manager should have made some kind of peace offering since the staff had failed to let you know in advance about the tipping policy. By admitting a mistake and making amends, she could have kept your patronage (which would be good for her business) and created a pleasant ending to an unfortunate experience (which would be good for you). Here is yet another example of why taking the high road isn't just the right thing to do; it's a good business move.

IS IT OKAY TO KEEP FREEBIES?

Q: *I recently received a roll of address labels from a company soliciting my business. I didn't ask for the labels, but since I've decided not to order from the company, is it wrong for me to use the ones I've received?*

A: Not at all. In fact, it would be wrong for you to throw them out, since we have a moral obligation not to be wasteful. It would be one thing if you ordered the labels on credit and used them but decided not to pay the bill. That is theft. Since you did not ask for these goods, however, there is no reason why you should not make use of them. Waste not, want not—and be glad for the freebies you get from marketers.

WHERE SHOULD I DRAW THE LINE WITH A CLIENT'S UNFAIR DEMANDS?

Q: *I am a literary agent in a large firm. One of my authors—let's call her Hazel (not her real name)—has been waiting patiently for a large advance check, and although we were expecting it some time ago and the publisher assured us it had been sent, the check hadn't turned up. Last week I discovered that an intern had misfiled the check and put it in the "slush pile," where we normally put manuscripts and other documents that we intend to read in the coming weeks. It was an innocent mistake, but Hazel was quite upset when I told her what had happened, and she told me that the intern should be fired. She even implied that if I didn't let the intern go, she would seek representation from another agent. I don't want to lose this VIP client, but on the other hand,*

I believe the punishment should fit the crime, and letting the intern go strikes me as a harsh response to what he did. What do you think?

A: Goodbye and good riddance—to Hazel. Your clients, even the powerful ones who supply a substantial portion of your yearly revenue, do not have a right to tell you how to run your affairs. It is understandable that Hazel would be upset in having to wait an extra week to get paid, but suggesting that the intern be fired seems more like a displacement of her anger than an attempt to find the right solution to the problem. It is also hard to see how a well-heeled author like Hazel was harmed by a small delay in receiving her advance. What happened to her is more of a nuisance than an injustice.

Instead of throwing the intern away like a used tissue, why not help the intern learn how to do his job more effectively? It is almost always better to respond to a mistake with compassion and kindness than with hostility. Besides, the intern is providing unpaid or inexpensive labor, and even if he gets some benefit out of the relationship (e.g., college credit, inside knowledge of the publishing industry), he is surely making an important contribution to the office. The lessons that he learns from you in how to respond effectively and ethically to mistakes will be more important in the long run than the knowledge he gains about the goings-on in a literary agent's workplace.

Any client who would deliver the ultimatum "him or me" in response to an innocent mistake is someone you may very well be better off without. Call her bluff and let her know that the standard you use to make decisions is fairness, not self-interest.

IS IT UNETHICAL TO MOVIE-HOP?

Q: *Going to the movies these days means visiting the local Cineplex with twenty-five screens. If I go early enough in the day, I can usually auditorium-hop and see two or three movies for the price of a single ticket. Since the film industry is a multibillion dollar business, I see nothing wrong with what I'm doing. I mean, the seat I'm taking would go empty if I didn't sit there. Whom does this harm?*

A: It harms the film business, the theater owner, your fellow patrons, and you. Theft is taking something that doesn't belong to you, so your practice makes you a thief. When you enter a theater to which you have not paid an admission fee, you're cheating the other people who paid their hard-earned money to be there. How do you think they would react if they knew you're getting something for nothing, while they paid as much as ten dollars? Imagine if everyone followed your lead and jumped from theater to theater. The people who bought tickets (i.e., the honest folks in the house) wouldn't get to see their movie, and that wouldn't be fair. In other words, the only way your ruse works is if only a small number of people do it. But why should the rules that apply to the rest of us not apply to you?

You're not just cheating other people by taking the low road. When we do the wrong thing (and despite your words to the contrary, surely you know what you're doing is wrong), we diminish ourselves. Even the seemingly innocuous practice of auditorium-hopping in the Cineplex damages our souls.

IS IT OKAY TO KEEP INCORRECT CHANGE?

Q: *A clerk at a local discount store was extremely rude to me the other day, and then she accidentally gave me twenty dollars too much in change. I kept it, because I figured it served her right. Do you agree?*

A: No, I don't. The money you received doesn't belong to you. Besides, the clerk could be fired for coming up short, and surely that punishment doesn't fit the crime.

Better to return the cash and tell the clerk how she made you feel. Chances are she was just having a bad day and will sincerely apologize. If she does not, it might be a good idea to let the manager know what you experienced. No business wants to have surly help on its staff. By giving the money back, you'll have twenty fewer dollars, but you'll sleep better at night knowing that you did the right thing.

SHOULD I REPORT A COWORKER FOR OFFICE THEFT?

Q: *The other day I stayed at work late to finish up a project at my office. Everyone had gone home except for the office manager. As I was preparing to leave, I noticed that she was taking a few bills from the petty cash box and placing them in her purse. She saw that I was on to her, and she begged me not to say anything to the supervisor. She explained that her ex-husband has been delinquent with his child support payments, and she promised to replace the money after we get paid in a few days. I told her I would think about it. What should I do?*

A: Your coworker intentionally committed a crime, and in so doing, she has undermined the trust that others place in her. Accordingly, you cannot take her at her word that she will repay the money, and if you say nothing and your boss learns that you knew about the theft and did nothing, you will be held partially accountable, and rightly so. After all, someone who steals once may very well steal again, and you were in a position to break the cycle by calling the matter to your supervisor's attention. It is not too late to do so, however. The fact that you needed some time to think about the matter simply shows that you are a person of conscience who is faced with a tough decision. On the one hand, you don't want to get a coworker in trouble. Who does? On the other hand, you have a duty to your employer and to your company's clients, who are the ultimate victims of your coworker's misdeed.

Even if it is true that your coworker is experiencing financial problems (and you cannot be certain that this is the case), this does not justify stealing from the company. If she really needs an advance on her paycheck, she could always make arrangements with personnel. You might now choose to go back to her and explain that you cannot keep what you witnessed to yourself. If she says, "Okay, I'll tell the boss myself; you don't have to get involved any further," it would still be wrong for you to keep quiet. How would you know whether or not she made good on her promise? Whether or not you talk with her directly, you are ethically obligated to report what you saw to your boss. He has a right to know about crimes committed in the workplace, and since you are the only witness, you are the one upon whose shoulders the burden falls to come forward.

No one likes to turn in a coworker, but you have a moral duty to do so, simply because you witnessed something that was both illegal and unethical.

By the way, companies can make it easier on employees in your situation by making it clear through written policies and employee orientation sessions that anyone who witnesses theft or other acts of wrongful conduct has a duty to report the incident to her supervisor. That way, you will know that you are acting in accordance with what is expected of you and will be free of the kind of hand-wringing that gave rise to your dilemma.

HOW SHOULD I DEAL WITH MY UNETHICAL BOSS?

Q: *I'm a secretary in a small company. My boss, who is not the owner of the firm, frequently asks me to get petty cash for him, and I know that he uses this money for personal expenses. It bothers me that he does this and implicates me in his schemes, but I'm a single mother, and I can't afford to lose my job. What should I do?*

A: As Edmund Burke said, "The only thing necessary for the triumph of evil is for good [people] to do nothing." It is understandable that you don't want to make waves, but your boss is doing something he shouldn't, and if you process those petty cash slips, you become part of the problem. Petty cash ultimately comes from clients, so your boss is a thief. You not only have a right to refuse to participate; you have a moral obligation to do so. You cannot be fired for standing up for yourself. Conversely, by taking the low road, you'll do everyone a disservice: the clients, your employer (which has put its trust in you), your boss (who needs to be stopped), and, ultimately, yourself. If your boss continues to make these inappropriate requests, you will have no alternative but to contact the person above him and let her know what is going on. It may also be possible to get personnel or human resources involved instead of your boss's boss.

IS IT WRONG TO DATE AN EMPLOYEE?

Q: *I'm the vice president for sales in a large pharmaceutical company. A few weeks ago we hired a group of recent college graduates to join our sales force. I'm very attracted to one of the new reps, and I know she's attracted to me. Would it be wrong to ask her out?*

A: Yes, it would. First, you can't be sure that she's attracted to you. She may simply be showing respect for your position of authority, and you could be wrongly interpreting this as personal interest. But even if it's clear that there is a mutual attraction, it's also true that there is an imbalance of power between the two of you. Should a romance fizzle out, she could find working with you intimidating, and everyone would then lose out: you, her, clients, and the company. Even if your organization does not have a policy prohibiting office romances, these liaisons are not a wise idea. Better to keep a sharp distinction between professional and personal life; in the long run, everyone will be better off.

SHOULD MY DATE HAVE OFFERED TO PAY?

Q: *I met a woman at a bar recently and asked her out on a date. She accepted and suggested that we go to a new place in town for dinner. It turns out that it was a very expensive place, and I don't make a lot of money. She, on the other hand, is a successful investment banker. When the check arrived, she didn't offer to help me pay for the meal, and it cost a lot of money. Do you think it was wrong of her not to suggest splitting the check?*

A: No. It would have been gracious of her to do so, but it was not ethically required. After all, you are the one who asked her out, and the rule of dating, which seems fair, is that the person who does the asking does the paying, at least for the first date. Perhaps it wasn't the kindest move on her part to propose an expensive restaurant for your first outing, but depending on how you presented yourself, she may have concluded that the two of you were similarly situated financially.

The fact that you have a disparity in your incomes that has already caused you some grief does not bode well for your future together, unless you're able to have an open and honesty conversation about money. Had you researched the restaurant proposal before the date, you would have discovered that it was in the expensive category, and then you could have proposed an alternative. You could have mentioned that the price was prohibitive for you, and then a red flag might have gone up for her. That wouldn't be such a bad thing, and in the long run could prove to be beneficial: If she is looking for someone who is more well-to-do than you are, it is better to find out now than a few weeks or months down the road, when both of you have invested your time and perhaps your feelings in the relationship.

Bottom line: The person who asks for the date pays for it. A truthful discussion earlier rather than later about the things that matter is both ethically appropriate and good "damage control."

HOW CAN WE KEEP OUR DIFFERENT TASTES FROM COMING BETWEEN US?

Q: *My wife insists on playing country music, which I hate, in the mornings. I'm into classic rock. We have vicious fights over who controls the stereo, and as stupid as it seems, it's beginning to adversely affect our relationship. I don't think it's fair that she dictates what we listen to before work, and she says the same about me. How can we break the impasse?*

A: You're right; it is stupid to ruin a relationship because of different tastes in music. But I wonder if the arguments are about something else. The master teacher of screenwriting Robert McKee writes in his book *Story: Substance, Structure, Style, and the Principles of Screenwriting*, "What is said and done is not what is thought and felt. The scene is not about what it seems to be about." That is, in the best screenplays, the characters don't say what they mean, or they don't mean what they say, so we shouldn't take their words at face value. Similarly, I believe, chronic fights over something as relatively petty as music choices are really about something deeper that may be harder to confront.

Life Principle #4 entails that neither you nor your wife should have the ultimate control over the airspace you share. Only an irrational person could disagree with such an obvious statement. But, as we all know, love is irrational, so you would do well to get some counseling, or at least be willing to have an open and honest conversation about what is truly bothering each of you.

WOULDN'T IT BE FAIR TO SHARE THE HOUSEWORK?

Q: *My husband refuses to do chores around the house. He says that his work is so demanding (he works in construction) that he has no energy in the evening to take out the trash, do the dishes, etc. The thing is, I have a job, too (I run a day care center), and while it may not be as physically demanding as building houses, I'm exhausted at the end of the day too. It feels like I really have two jobs: working with kids all day, and caring for my husband at night. It seems unfair to me, but my husband argues he makes most of the money for the household, so I should get off his case. Who is right?*

A: You are. Your husband might have a point if

you spent your days watching television and eating chocolate-covered cherries, but both of you have demanding jobs that leave each person drained at the end of the day. If your husband thinks that running a day care center is easier than putting up drywall, ask him to take your place for a day. I suspect he'll be glad to get back to the construction site.

It's not a contest, however, as to who has the more physically taxing line of work. Life Principle #4 requires that work be distributed equitably at home. "Equitably" does not necessarily mean "equally." Just as it should not be a contest as to who has the more taxing line of work, neither should it be a matter of dispute who has to do more around the house. You both live there, so both of you should contribute to its maintenance. You cook, he cleans. Or the other way around.

The central theme of this book is that it is in our own interests to do the right thing. Your husband is more likely to enjoy a satisfying relationship with you if he takes an active role in the operation of the household. That isn't the reason that he should pitch in (the reason is that it's the right thing to do), but it is a welcome consequence of doing so. He rolls up his sleeves during the day to earn a paycheck; he should do the same on the home front. Fairness requires nothing less.

SHOULD MY MOM HAVE TO JUSTIFY HER ARGUMENTS?

Q: *My name is Brian, and I'm in the fifth grade. When my mom and I have an argument, she always ends the discussion by saying, "You just have to do what I say because I'm your mother." I don't think that's a good enough reason. It's not fair for her to expect me to do something just because I happen to be her son. What do you think?*

A: When you're ten years old, that statement is as good a reason as any, and better than most. Still, you might want to press your mom—respectfully, of course—for more in the way of justification. It would be good of her to offer one.

For example, if she tells you to get a haircut but you just don't see the need for it, she might say, "Rightly or wrongly, people judge you by your appearance. By taking pride in how you look, you will command respect, and you will also feel better about yourself." You still might balk at the monthly trip to the barber—I know I did when I was your age—but at least you'll know why you have to go.

Bottom line: While you are in her care, when the two of you have a disagreement she has the moral authority to offer any justification she cares to—or none at all. After all, she's your mother!

DID I DESERVE TO BE FIRED?

Q: *I'm a lifeguard at a community swimming pool, and the job supports me while I work my way through a local college. Last week a kid went to the bathroom in the pool under my watch, but instead of closing down the pool, which we're required to do, I just cleaned up the mess and kept the pool open. The main reason I did so is that a lot of the kids at the pool told me that they didn't care about the accident; they came a long way to enjoy a swim. My supervisor found out about what I did and fired me. I think he was wrong, since I was trying to keep everyone happy. This is what I get for being a nice guy! What do you think?*

A: There are four moral values at stake in this scenario: keeping promises (since you signed a contract with the pool obligating you to follow their rules), preventing harm (since defecating in a pool poses a public health hazard), benefiting the community (since the community you serve, or at least a significant proportion thereof, wanted to enjoy the pool), and being fair (the punishment should fit the crime). In firing you, your boss is placing the greatest importance on following the rules of the organization to the letter. He may be right, but assuming that you've been a good employee in general, letting you go seems unfair, particularly since your goal was not to make life easy for yourself but to benefit others. By strongly reprimanding you but keeping you on the staff, he would have honored his commitment to the community and helped you to become a better lifeguard. Unfortunately, everyone now loses out with his excessive response to your mistake in judgment. If taking the high road is a win-win proposition, meting out punishment unfairly is a lose-lose one.

HOW CAN I TEACH MY NIECE THAT TWO WRONGS DON'T MAKE A RIGHT?

Q: *My fifteen-year-old niece found a diamond ring under the stove in her mother's home. (They are only the second family to live in this home.) The assumption was made that the ring belonged to the previous owner of the home. Her father (my brother, who does not live in this home) explained to my niece that sometimes the sentimental value of something far surpasses the monetary value, and the right thing to do is to at least make an attempt to find out if the ring belongs to the previous owner. Her mother knows how to get in touch with the previous owner but refuses to give my niece her name and number because she didn't like something that occurred during the real estate transaction when she bought the home from them. She told my niece to keep the ring. They had the ring appraised (eight hundred dollars) and kept it.*

My niece felt caught in the middle, and since she depended on her mother for the contact information, she just did what she was told. My brother and I, on the other hand, agree that whatever happened during the real estate transaction should not have any influence at all on whether or not the attempt should be made to return the ring.

I hope you will be able to assist us in teaching my niece that there are times when you just have to do put your feelings aside and do what is right.

A: The fact that your niece's mother had a beef with the owner of the diamond ring is ethically irrelevant in deciding how to dispose of the diamond ring. From an ethical perspective, there is no justification in keeping something that doesn't belong to us, whether that "thing" is a valuable piece of jewelry or a six-pack of soda that one finds in a shopping cart in the grocery store parking lot. Life Principle #4, Be Fair, requires, among other things, that we make a reasonable effort to return items that come into our possession that belong to someone else. In this case, it will take little effort to apply the principle.

Who knows? Perhaps your niece's actions will move the owner of the ring to reconsider her treatment of your niece's mother. Only the hardest of hearts would fail to be warmed by a gesture that other people might not have had the integrity to make. Whether or not desirable consequences flow from the return of the ring, however, that action is the right one to take.

With respect to putting one's feeling aside, the fifth and final Life Principle, Be Loving, asks us to develop a loving attitude toward friend and foe alike. With friends this is not a problem, but it's almost impossible to do when dealing with someone who has treated us disrespectfully, as your niece's mother feels was the case in her business transaction. However, the goal of becoming an ethical human being ultimately means developing the right feelings so that we are moved to act appropriately.

LIFE PRINCIPLE #5
BE LOVING

Hate's goin' round breaking many hearts
Stop it please before it's gone too far
—Stevie Wonder, "Love's in Need of Love Today"

The fifth and final Life Principle is rarely found in traditional books on ethics. There you will see plenty of discussion of rights and responsibilities, of justice and fairness, of duties to keep one's promises and to avoid harming others. The Life Principles of Do No Harm, Make Things Better, Respect Others, and Be Fair are the foundation of any and all moral systems, and they are found in every religion and culture that has ever existed or is likely to exist. We cannot imagine a society that would not place these notions front and center, whether codified in the law or taught by parents and in Sunday school. But if the moral life were made up only of allegiance to these principles, it would be a pretty barren one indeed.

Where Life Principles #1–4 are obligatory, Life Principle #5, Be Loving, might best be considered "above and beyond the call of duty." To be loving to one's neighbor is an ideal to which we should aspire, but if we fail to act lovingly to those with whom we come into contact, we can hardly be considered unethical (unless your job is to love people, which raises ethical and legal questions of its own, at least outside of Nevada).

Can we be faulted by failing to prevent harm to others when doing so would take little effort? Yes; Life Principle #1 requires this of us. If a friend of yours has just lost her mother, Life Principle #2 asks that you console your friend, even if it is uncomfortable for you to do so. If you pass along a rumor you have heard about a neighbor, you have violated Life Principle #3. But it seems a stretch to suggest that we err by not loving the annoying coworker, the crazy driver who cuts us off on the highway, or the lazy clerk at the grocery store. Might it make sense to create a place for love in the moral framework that is the Life Principles? Let's take a closer look.

Recognizing Various Definitions and Portrayals of Love

Here are top ten popular songs, according to *Billboard*, for the week ending January 29, 2005:

(1) "Let Me Love You," Mario

(2) "I Don't Want to Be," Gavin DeGraw

(3) "Step," Ciara featuring Missy Elliott

(4) "Over and Over," Nelly featuring Tim McGraw

(5) "Beautiful Soul," Jesse McCartney

(6) "Since U Been Gone," Kelly Clarkson

(7) "Soldier," Destiny's Child featuring T.I. and Lil' Wayne

(8) "Drop It Like It's Hot," Snoop Dogg featuring Pharrell

(9) "True," Ryan Cabrera

(10) "Breakaway," Kelly Clarkson

Here is the top-ten list for the week ending five years before the previous list:

(1) "I Knew I Loved You," Savage Garden

(2) "What a Girl Wants," Christina Aguilera

(3) "Smooth," Santana featuring Rob Thomas

(4) "Back at One," Brian McKnight
(5) "Bring It All to Me," Blaque
(6) "Blue (Da Ba Dee)," Eiffel 65
(7) "Hot Boyz," Missy "Misdemeanor" Elliott featuring Nas and Eve
(8) "That's the Way It Is," Celine Dion
(9) "I Need to Know," Marc Anthony
(10) "My Love Is Your Love," Whitney Houston

And here is the list for the week ending fifteen years before the first list:

(1) "How Am I Supposed to Live Without You," Michael Bolton
(2) "Opposites Attract," Paula Abdul (duet with the Wild Pair)
(3) "Downtown Train," Rod Stewart
(4) "Two to Make It Right," Seduction
(5) "Janie's Got a Gun," Aerosmith
(6) "I Remember You," Skid Row
(7) "Free Fallin'," Tom Petty
(8) "Pump Up the Jam," Technotronic
(9) "Just Between You and Me," Lou Gramm
(10) "Everything," Jody Watley [1]

---

[1] Source: www.billboard.com

Almost every song in this fifteen-year span concerns love, but a specific kind of love: that between romantic partners. We see a similar obsession in popular movies, magazines, books, and television shows. What's more, American popular culture has become one of our most widely exported commodities. Travel anywhere in the world and you will hear many of the same songs, see many of the same movies and TV programs, and read many of the same romance novels that you find in your hometown. It is difficult to grow up anywhere in the world and not believe that "love" means "a burning desire to be linked forever with another person."

It was not always this way. There were four words for "love" in ancient Greek:

(1)   *Eros*, from which we get "erotic," and which gives rise to most of the pop songs above

(2)   *Storge*, or love between parent and child

(3)   *Agape*, or Godly love

(4)   *Philos*, the love of, well, everything else

It is worth noting, however, as explained in the *Wikipedia* encyclopedia, that "with Greek as with many other languages, it has been historically difficult to separate the meanings of these words totally, and so we can find examples of *agape* being used with much the same meaning as *eros*. At the same time the ancient Greek text of the Bible has examples of the verb *agapo* being used with the same meaning as *phileo*." (See http://en.wikipedia.org/wiki/Love for more on this.)

Philos is the root of such words as philosophy (the love of wisdom), philology (the love of words), and philanthropy (literally, the love of people). Philadelphia, the City of Brotherly Love, takes its name from this Greek root, and the great philharmonic orchestras are so named because they are "lovers of harmony." Bibliophiles love books, cinephiles love movies, and audiophiles are passionately devoted to the best reproductions of music because they are in love with the purity of sound. There are as many different *kinds* of love as there are things to *be* loved.

In my view, the most perceptive analysis of love is that offered by psychoanalyst Erich Fromm in *The Art of Loving*. For Fromm, love involves not sacrificing ourselves for someone else or demanding that others give selflessly to us. Rather, the goal of love is to create an environment in which each person in the relationship can be the best he or she can be:

Respect is not fear and awe; it denotes, in accordance with the root of the word (*respicere*

= to look at), the ability to see a person as he is, to be aware of his unique individuality. Respect means the concern that the other person should grow and unfold as he is. Respect, thus, implies the absence of exploitation. I want the loved person to grow and unfold for his own sake, and in his own ways, and not for the purpose of serving me. If I love the other person, I feel one with him or her, but with him as he is, not as I need him to be as an object for my use. It is clear that respect is possible only if I have achieved independence; if I can stand and walk without needing crutches, without having to dominate and exploit anyone else. Respect exists only on the basis of freedom: "*l'amour est l'enfant de la liberté*" as an old French song says; love is the child of freedom, never that of domination.[2]

It is not an accident that this description of love draws on Life Principle #3, for it is impossible to imagine a loving relationship that is not based on mutual respect.

In contrast to the way love is portrayed in popular

[2] Erich Fromm, *The Art of Loving*, (New York: Perennial Classics, 1956), pp. 26–27.

culture (as either a frenzied state of body and mind or a feeling that is impossible to sustain), this notion of love is both practical and enriching. Viewed this way, it is easy to understand why love is rightly to be considered the fifth and final Life Principle. Each principle expresses an idea about human relationships that is worth taking seriously both for the sake of other people and for ourselves. The Life Principles provide a framework for answering life's toughest questions. They give us guidance when we are not sure how to act or which choice we should make. As we've discussed, troubling situations call upon us to answer the following questions:

(1) Which choice will avoid causing harm to others, minimize the harm that is unavoidable, or prevent harm that is reasonably foreseeable?

(2) Which choice will make things better?

(3) Which choice evinces respect for others?

(4) Which choice is the most fair?

With Life Principle #5, we add a fifth and final question to our moral checklist:

(5) What is the loving thing to do?

Integrating Life Principle #5 by Starting with Self Love

In discussing how she learned to manage her fluctuating weight, Oprah Winfrey said, "I wasn't able to get my weight under control until I began to treat myself the way I treat others." Ethics, as we have noted, is about taking the rights and well being of others at least as seriously as we take our own interests. Oprah's statement, however, reveals that many of us, perhaps women in particular, often value other people more than we value ourselves. Just as it is wrong to be selfish in the extreme, it is wrong to exist solely for the benefit of other people. Even saints must take care of their own needs, if for no other reason than without so doing, they cannot be of service to others. If Mother Teresa had neglected her health, she would not have been able to minister to the sick and needy for so long. The love of others must begin with the love of self.

It is a sad feature of our nature that we will often do or say things to ourselves that we would never consider doing or saying to other people.

We choose food for ourselves that we know isn't good for us.

We choose boyfriends or girlfriends, husbands or

wives, lovers or "soul mates" we wouldn't wish on our worst enemies.

We allow clutter to accumulate in our living or work space.

We fail to exercise, in spite of knowing that exercise is essential for maintaining physical and mental health (or, at the opposite end of the spectrum, we push ourselves to the extreme).

We engage in negative self-talk throughout the day, even though we would never talk to our friends or family this way.

We obsess over what we should have done or fantasize about what we'd like to achieve while doubting we could ever get there.

In short, we fail to love ourselves. And that's not just unfortunate. It's unethical.

Ethics is *not* solely about our relationships with lovers, bosses, assistants, and the community at large. It is also about our relationships with ourselves, not just because we cannot benefit others if we don't take care of ourselves, but because we owe it to ourselves to treat ourselves with respect.

The best way to apply Life Principle #5 is to keep Life Principles #1–4 in mind at all times and apply them to our own lives.

When we play in our minds that endless tape loop of negative self-talk, we violate Life Principle #1, Do No Harm. It harms our souls to speak poorly of ourselves.

When we choose a steady diet of junk food over healthful meals, we violate Life Principle #2, Make Things Better. The scope of "things" should not be limited to those persons, places, and inanimate objects outside of us.

When we dishonor our conscience, say by keeping quiet when we know we should speak out, we violate Life Principle #3, Respect Others.

Since we have the same intrinsic value that others do, it is unfair, and thus a violation of Life Principle #4, to deny ourselves that to which we are entitled.

Let us now consider how we might broaden the scope of Life Principle #5 and think of what it might mean, in practical terms, to be loving to others each day of our lives.

Learning to Love Others

Every modern best-selling book about improving sales, negotiating successfully, and becoming a top manager owes an enormous debt of gratitude to Dale Carnegie's 1936 book, *How to Win Friends and Influence People.* Indeed, it is hard to think of a single self-help book that isn't based on the insights of this visionary work. The theme of *Life Principles*, too, has its roots in Carnegie's philosophy, which is that being genuinely interested in other people is a sure way to become successful professionally and personally. Although I am taking great pains to emphasize that personal gain is a wonderful consequence, not the primary reason, to be concerned with how we treat other people, both Carnegie and I seek to dispel the popular notion that taking the high road is inconsistent with enriching oneself. Ethical conduct is not only consistent with winning in every aspect of one's life—it is instrumental to doing so.

No one before or since Carnegie has written so eloquently yet simply about the small but powerful ways we can make positive differences in the lives of other people. He doesn't put it in these terms, but Carnegie's strategies for "winning friends and influencing people" are actually ways of showing our love for the people in our lives.

Some of Carnegie's strategies are so basic that it is easy to overlook their forcefulness. I'd like to invite you to examine the following list closely. Can you honestly say you do these things with your friends, family, and coworkers? Do you see the benefits to other people that each rule offers? Can you imagine how taking each rule seriously would enrich you, too?

(1) Smile.
(2) Begin in a friendly way.
(3) Don't criticize, condemn, or complain.
(4) Give honest and sincere appreciation.
(5) Become genuinely interested in other people.
(6) Remember that a person's name is to that person the sweetest and most important sound in any language.
(7) Be a good listener. Encourage others to talk about themselves.
(8) Talk in terms of the other person's interests.
(9) Make the other person feel important—and do it sincerely.
(10) The only way to get the best of an argument is to avoid it.
(11) Show respect for the other person's opinions. Never say, "You're wrong."
(12) If you are wrong, admit it quickly and emphatically.
(13) Let the other person do a great deal of the talking.
(14) Try honestly to see things from the other person's point of view.
(15) Be sympathetic with the other person's ideas and desires.

These rules have one thing in common: All require us

to get outside of ourselves and think about how our actions will affect other people. This is the essence of ethics, and it is why being loving should rightly be considered a Life Principle.

Applying Life Principle #5 in Everyday Life

HOW CAN I PUT MY CONSCIENCE AT EASE?

Q: *I am haunted by something I did a long time ago. My parents and I were visiting a fancy restaurant in France, and I noticed that a glass showcase in the lobby displayed artifacts related to the restaurant. While my parents were finishing the meal, I went out the lobby to look at the showcase, and I opened the panel to look more closely at a small sculpture. When I closed the panel, my sweater caught on the sculpture and knocked it over, smashing it to bits. In horror I ran back to my parents but didn't tell them what happened for fear that they would be angry with me. I was a freshman in high school at the time, and I am now a senior, but I never told anyone what I did, and I feel terrible that I broke something that may have been very valuable. What should I do?*

A: First, let yourself off the hook. Everyone makes mistakes, and it is good that your mistake bothered you at the time, since a guilty conscience shows that you are rightly concerned with how your actions affect others. What troubles me about your letter is that you felt unable to tell your parents what happened. Since they cared enough about you to take you overseas and treat you to a nice meal, why do you think they would be merciless in their response to you? Surely they would see that you didn't mean any harm by your actions. Letting your parents know about the mishap would also have given them the chance to offer to pay the restaurant owner for the damage. Since the accident occurred several years ago, it is probably forgotten by now, so you should put this unfortunate event out of your mind. You might want to write the restaurant owner a letter and tell him that you feel bad about what you did and ask if there is anything you can do to right the wrong.

Second, it is hard to believe that a restaurant, even a four-star one in France, would put an invaluable artifact in a display case, so your accident surely did not cause irreparable harm. But I hope that you can find a way to give yourself a break and also to tell your parents about the incident. I would be very surprised if your parents did not take your pain to heart and help you find a way to make peace with yourself. It is wrong to continue to punish yourself for an innocent mistake from so long ago. Life Principle #5 applies not just to how we treat others, but to how we treat ourselves, too.

HOW SHOULD I HANDLE MY UNPLEASANT RELATIVE?

Q: *A close relative of mine has personal traits that really get on my nerves. He is not merely rude; at family get-togethers he says things to me that are downright hurtful. I've tried ignoring him, but I feel bad when I do that. He is a part of my family, after all. It seems like a situation I can't win; I don't like it when I write him off, but he gets my goat so often that I just can't stand it. What should I do?*

A: Your relative would do well to honor Life Principle #3, Respect Others. However, you cannot write another person's script; feeling that you can do so is a recipe for unhappiness. You have a right to be treated with respect, even—or especially—from a close family member. Life Principle #5, Be Loving, has an important role for you to play in your relationship with this person. Part of what it means to be a loving person, as the excerpt from Erich Fromm's *The Art of Loving* showed earlier, is to accept others as they are. This does not mean putting up with abuse; you can and should make your feelings known and ask him to rethink his behavior. But that doesn't go far enough. Put yourself in his position. What would motivate a family member to be unkind to another member of the clan? How might his own insecurities or feelings of inadequacy be shaping his behavior? This is an attempt not to excuse churlish behavior but rather to understand what is giving rise to it. After all, understanding is the first step toward acceptance.

If it is the case that this man really loves you but has an unfortunate way of showing it, then it may be worthwhile to overlook some less-than-savory aspects of what he brings to the table. Surely you have unpleasant qualities that get on other people's nerves, yet those who care about you accept them as part of the whole package. As challenging as loving this man may be, the alternative—erasing him from your life—is worse, as your own experience has shown.

WHAT CAN I DO ABOUT MY UN-NEIGHBORLY NEIGHBORS?

Q: *I live in an apartment, and my next-door neighbors have three children who are loud and obnoxious. It's not really the children's fault that they're so misbehaved; the blame lies with the parents, who never seem to discipline their children. They let the kids run up and down the halls yelling at the top of their lungs. I've complained to the management, and the problem subsides for a while and then rears its ugly head again. I've gotten to the point where I send nasty vibes to the family whenever I have the misfortune of running into them in the elevator or the hallway. When the mailman accidentally delivers their mail to my box, I throw it away. I don't like being this way, but I feel I'm entitled to have a decent quality of life, and these people are making it hard to do so. I don't want to move; why should I? I like where I live and don't feel like going through the hassle of finding a new apartment. How should I deal with these unpleasant people?*

A: You are indeed entitled to be free from undue disturbances in your apartment. Noisy neighbors interfere with your right to enjoy a peaceful existence. You did the right thing to let the manager know what's going on. It is not surprising, however, that this didn't solve the problem. Short of evicting the family, which is hard to do, there isn't much they can do besides put the offenders on notice.

If you can't attack the source of the problem, the only alternative is to find another way to cope with it. This means an attitude adjustment. How does it make you feel to turn off your normally sunny disposition when you encounter the family? Not very good, by your own admission. How, then, could this be the right course of action to take? You might very well benefit by keeping Life Principle #5 front and center. Befriend the family. Get the kids a toy. Offer to help the parents in some way, perhaps by delivering errant mail to them personally, as opposed to committing a crime by tossing it in the trash. Open your heart and be generous. Besides being welcome to the recipients, this attitude is more likely to get you what you want: peace. If your neighbors see that you care about them, they will be more likely to take your concerns to heart. It is an axiom of human nature that we are motivated to please those who please us.

Conversely, it is easy to write off someone who treats us with disrespect or contempt. Take the high road. Follow the example that Warren Haynes sings about with the Allman Brothers Band and let your soul shine. You'll feel better about yourself, and you'll be more likely to create the kind of environment you want to have. Oh, and you'll be doing good for others, too.

By the way, did you ever stop to consider the things *you* do that might annoy your neighbors and why you should avoid doing these things?

HOW SHOULD I RESPOND TO POOR CUSTOMER SERVICE?

Q: *I live in a small town, and one of the clerks in the grocery store where I shop is frequently nasty to me. I don't know why she has such a lousy attitude. I consider myself a friendly person, but this woman really pushes my buttons. Whenever I'm unlucky enough to get her, I avoid making pleasant conversation and usually make a cell phone call to pass the time. Should I tell the manager or write him an anonymous note about this irritating employee? I feel like I have an obligation to let the store know what's going on; they could be losing business because of this clerk with an attitude. However, I don't like the idea of getting people in trouble, or even fired. What do you say?*

A: Customers in particular, and people in general, have a right to be treated with respect. It is odd to encounter a perpetual grouch in service occupations, since it in the employee's own interest to treat customers decently. Doing otherwise is a legitimate basis for dismissal. Still, there is the ideal world in which everyone does what they should, and then there is the world in which we live. Although unethical conduct provides ethicists with work, it is understandable that you and others in your situation bridle at being on the receiving end of it.

Since a corollary of Life Principle #4, Be Fair, calls for you to stand up to injustice, you would certainly be within your rights to bring the matter to the attention of the manager. You are also right to be concerned about the consequences of your actions, since this move could very well penalize the errant worker, if not lead to her getting a pink slip. Is there another way of handling the matter, one with less dire consequences?

Yes there is, and Life Principle #5 shows the way. By meeting nastiness with love rather than with righteous anger, you can avoid the guilt you'd feel in being the catalyst for getting this woman fired. Perhaps she is a single mother who depends on this work to care for her children. Why not talk with her privately and share your concerns with her? There could be a lot of reasons why she is acting this way, and she may very well be unaware of how her attitude is affecting others. Reading her the riot act isn't the way to go during this chat; rather, using the "praise sandwich" technique of giving criticism is more likely to be effective.

This technique involves three steps:

(1) Begin with something flattering but sincere. Say, for example, "I'd like you to know that I

appreciate all of the hard work you do for us here." Besides being a nice thing in and of itself, this will lower her guard and make her receptive to the rest of what you have to say.

(2) Bring up your concerns, but by using "I" rather than "you" language. Saying something like, "You should know that your lousy attitude is really annoying" will only put her on the defensive, even (or especially) if it comes from the heart. Instead, say, "I'm sure you're not aware of it, but I notice that frequently you aren't very polite. I'm not sure what I've done to warrant this, but I wanted you to know that I would appreciate it if you could speak to me the way you'd like someone to speak to you." No one can legitimately take issue with a statement that flows from your own perception and experience.

(3) End by affirming your faith in her to do the right thing. You could say, for example, "You seem like a nice person, and I hope you'll take what I'm saying to heart."

By going to the clerk directly rather than going over her head, you at least give her the chance to be aware of the problem and to correct it. It most cases, this is all it will take to solve the matter. If that isn't the case, then you may have no choice but to bring the problem to the manager's attention. You could also take your business elsewhere, but the store should be given the chance to make things right. They don't want to lose you as a customer, and by doing something rather than nothing, you will be making the shopping experience more pleasant not only for yourself but for everyone else, too. And it takes so little effort, really, to accomplish that goal.

WHAT IS THE BEST WAY TO DEAL WITH AN ANNOYING COWORKER?

Q: *One of my colleagues has the worst attitude I've ever encountered in a workplace. She never has a nice thing to say to or about anyone, and she walks around all day with a scowl on her face. We work in a large space with semi-private cubicles, and it is easy to hear her complain from the time she gets to work until the time she leaves at the end of the day. I need this job and can't afford to give it up, but this woman really makes coming to work a drag. I know that an office isn't supposed to be a party atmosphere, and perhaps there are things going on in this person's private life that cause her to be so hostile, but I feel that she should leave her personal issues at home. After*

*all, everyone has problems, but being a responsible adult
means having a mature attitude at work, don't you think?
I would complain to the boss about her, but they are very
close, and I'm sure he would take her side and view me as
the problem. What should I do?*

A: The modern office design makes problematic coworkers like yours harder to deal with than they were
before. When everyone had his own private space, the
only time one had to confront an unpleasant colleague
was at the water cooler, in meetings, or in the elevator.
The open-air structure of most indoor work spaces
erodes the privacy we used to enjoy and forces us to
work cheek-to-jowl with people we'd rather avoid.

If it is impossible for you to relocate to a cubicle
far from the offending person, and it really is the case
that an appeal to the manager would be futile (a con-
clusion I would not jump to, since you never know
until you try), then it is up to you to make the necessary change from within. Ask yourself, "What kind of
a person is perpetually angry?" What is anger, anyway?
For many of us, anger is our way of protecting ourselves from being hurt. To understand what is behind
a particular behavioral trait, we might wonder what
the behavior accomplishes. Anger drives people away.

It creates fear or at least the desire to go elsewhere. Yet our natural desire is to bring people closer to us. Human beings are not solitary creatures; we seek closeness with others. Something has turned this woman's world upside down and caused her to treat people in way that perhaps she has been (and may continue to be) treated.

As Atticus Finch put it in Harper Lee's *To Kill a Mockingbird*, "You never really understand a person until you consider things from his point of view—until you climb into his skin and walk around in it." What if it is the case that this woman has no love in her life? I'm not talking about the absence of a romantic interest (though that may indeed be the case). I'm wondering if, more broadly, not a soul expresses any care or concern for her. You suggest that she is close to the manager, but that relationship may not have the "loving touch." What appears at first blush to be a nuisance to get rid of may instead be an opportunity for you to bring some joy into another person's life.

I propose that you consider making Life Principle #5 work for both you and her. Bring her a flower or some cookies. Ask her how she's doing. Smile. Take a genuine interest in her. It would not be surprising if her sourness turned, if only slightly, into something sweeter. Your primary purpose in showing her some loving kindness is not to make your life easier. It is to be compassionate to a person who appears to be in dire need of something positive in her life. Whatever happy consequences flow from your behavior are simply welcome side effects.

SOURCES OF
THE LIFE PRINCIPLES

Out of many, one.
**—Official motto of the United States,
from the Latin, *E pluribus unum*.**

In 1989, William F. Buckley, the creator and host of the PBS talk show *Firing Line*, interviewed Mother Teresa. He asked her why she devoted her life to helping the poor. Her response was, "I am simply doing God's work." Buckley seemed perplexed and obviously wanted a more detailed answer, perhaps the sort of lengthy response he himself would give to such a question, but Mother Teresa had nothing more to say on the subject.

To be a believer is to have a basis for justifying the five Life Principles. In *Oneness: Great Principles Shared by All Religions*, Jeffrey Moses shows the religious origins of the concepts represented by the Life Principles.

This is how three faiths construe Life Principle #1, Do
No Harm:

Hinduism
Do not hurt others, do no injury by thought or
deed, utter no word to pain thy fellow creatures.

Buddhism
Hurt none by word or deed.

Islam
There should be neither harm nor reciprocat-
ing of harm. [1]

Although the great religions take pains to say that one
should not expect anything in return when one gives
of oneself, they also note that following Life Principle
#2, Make Things Better, happens to provide good con-
sequences to all concerned:

Christianity
Give, and it shall be given unto you...For with
the same measure that ye mete withal it shall
be measured to you again.

---

[1] Jeffrey Moses, *Oneness: Great Principles Shared by All Religions*, Revised
and Expanded Edition (New York: Ballantine Books), pp. 22–23.

Judaism
Cast your bread upon the waters: for you will find it after many days.

Islam
Those who give in charity have lent to Allah a goodly loan.

Hinduism
Give, and your wealth shall grow; give, and you shall more safely keep the wealth you have. [2]

The duty to tell the truth is one of the applications of Life Principle #3, Respect Others. Here is the formulation of that duty in six religious or spiritual traditions:

Christianity
Putting away lying, speak every man truth with his neighbor: for we are members one of another.

Judaism
Speak ye every man truth to his neighbor; execute the judgment of truth…in your gates.

[2] Ibid, pp. 146–147.

Islam
Do not clothe the truth with falsehood; do not knowingly conceal the truth.

Hinduism
Say what is true! Do thy duty. Do not swerve from the truth.

Ashanti Proverb/African Wisdom
A lie can annihilate a thousand truths.

Confucianism
Sincerity is the way of heaven, and to think how to be sincere is the way of a man. Never was there one possessed of complete sincerity who did not move others. Never was there one without sincerity who was able to move others. [3]

What does it mean to honor Life Principle #4, Be Fair? The great religions speak to this:

Islam
Repay evil with good and, lo, he between whom and you there was enmity will become your warm friend.

[3] Ibid, pp. 65–66.

Hinduism
When one injures another, the injured turns around and injures the injurer. Similarly, when one cherishes another, the other cherishes the cherisher. One should frame one's rule of conduct according to this.

Buddhism
Conquer your foe by force, and you increase his anger. Conquer by love, and you will reap no after sorrow.

Confucianism
Confucius was asked, "What do you say of the remark, 'Repay enmity with kindness?'" And he replied, "How then would you repay kindness? Repay kindness with kindness, and enmity with justice." [4]

Life Principle #5, Be Loving, is the lifeblood of every faith:

Judaism
Thou shalt love thy neighbor as thyself.

---

[4] Ibid, pp. 10–11, 102.

Christianity

A new commandment I give to you, That you love one another; even as I have loved you.... By this all men will know that you are my disciples, if you have love for one another.

Hinduism

A man obtains a proper rule of action by looking on his neighbor as himself.

Confucianism

Seek to be in harmony with all your neighbors; live in amity with your brethren.

Islam

No one is a believer until he loves for his neighbor, and for his brother, what he loves for himself.

Buddhism

As water quenches the thirst of the good and the bad alike, and cleanses them of dust and impurity, so also shall you treat your friend and your foe alike with loving kindness. [5]

[5] Ibid, pp. 10–11, 102.

Persons of faith find the justification for the rightful conduct through sacred texts. One has a responsibility to avoid harming others, make things better, tell the truth, be fair, and treat others with loving kindness because God so commands. When asked, "Why do you tell the truth when it would be easier to lie?" a believer simply has to say, "Because God expects me to." She may, but need not, provide a justification beyond what is provided for in Scripture.

It is possible, however, to justify the Life Principles without reference to religious tradition. Philosophical theories such as those developed by Immanuel Kant and John Stuart Mill offer secular justifications for each of these principles. For example, Kant argues that all of us ought to act in ways that can and should be universalized—hence the duty to tell the truth, among many other moral duties. Mill was the proponent of a theory known as utilitarianism, which looks to the consequences of an act or moral rule to justify the existence of that act or rule.

Some persons of faith may balk at the idea that all religious traditions are founded on the same moral concepts. As the above excerpts from *Oneness* show, however, Christianity, Judaism, Buddhism, Hinduism, and other faiths express in their holy texts the ideas that I am calling the Life Principles. It is simply not the case that at their most fundamental level the great religions of the West and East espouse different notions of morality.

Since the terrorist attacks on the United States of September 11, 2001, some people have chosen to demonize Islam. But the fanatics who flew planes into the World Trade Center and the Pentagon were not applying the moral principles of the Islamic faith. By using religion to justify the murder of civilians, they were twisting a noble way of life into something ugly and hateful. Islam was not the source of the problem any more than Judaism was the cause of problems in the Weimar Republic in Germany following World War I. The divine spirit is a loving and forgiving one; it is human beings who take spiritual ideas and pervert them for our own ends. Religion isn't the problem; ignorance and hatred are.

CHALLENGES OF
THE LIFE PRINCIPLES

If I am not for myself, then who will be for me?
If I am only for myself, then what am I?
If not now, when?
—Rabbi Hillel

J ust as life is not without conflict, living by the Life
Principles presents challenges of its own. In this
chapter we'll consider how to deal with conflicts among
the principles. We'll also consider how to take the high
road when others don't, and what is required to make
the Life Principles second nature.

Finding Resolution When
Principles Conflict

The five Life Principles provide a framework for
addressing life's toughest challenges. When we are

considering a particular course of action, it behooves us to ask ourselves:

- ❖ Will this action harm someone or something? If so, what other course of action will allow me to avoid causing harm?
- ❖ Will this action make things better for all concerned? If not, what might do so? If so, is there another option that may bring even more benefits?
- ❖ Will this action be respectful of others?
- ❖ Will this action be fair?
- ❖ Will this action be a loving thing to do?

We often find ourselves faced with what appears to be a conflict among the Life Principles. When your friend asks you if you like her new dress, how can you be honest without hurting her feelings? When you notice a coworker doing something he shouldn't be doing, how can you respect your commitment to the company and not harm your relationship with your colleague? If you discover your daughter's diary and want to know why she has been acting so strangely lately, is it more important to honor her right to privacy or to read it, look for clues to her behavior, and thus take steps to protect her from harm?

As I hope I have shown through the question-and-answer sections of this book, there are few genuine ethical dilemmas where one is forced to rank the Life Principles in order of importance. With a little bit of mental effort—and, perhaps, through consultation with others—we can find creative ways to honor all of the Life Principles. Despite the media's attempt to portray ethical problems as dire situations in which one must choose one principle over another, the real world is much more complex, and answers to even the toughest questions need not make us compromise one principle to act upon another.

Nevertheless, we may very well find ourselves in situations in which we indeed must decide whether telling a lie is necessary to protect someone from being hurt, for example. If we do not have the luxury of time to consider all of the options that might be available, then indeed we may have to rank the Life Principles in order of importance. We certainly don't want to do so randomly or flip a coin to determine the right hierarchy. Why should fate or luck determine the outcome of an important decision? Still, on what basis might we legitimately rank-order the Life Principles?

Obviously, buying time is the best way to go if at all possible (and this is the case more often than we might think; it never hurts to ask someone for some time to make a choice that has significant consequences). But whether or not that option is available, there is one important thing we must keep in mind: There is no way to rank the Life Principles in order of importance independent of what the facts of the situation happen to be.

In other words, it is not always more important to be truthful than to avoid harming someone. If you were hiding a Jewish family in Nazi Germany and the Gestapo arrived at your door, would you be doing wrong by lying about what you were up to? Of course not. By the same token, however, sometimes it is more important to respect others than to avoid harming someone. Recall the scene in Martin Scorsese's *Raging Bull* in which Jake LaMotta, portrayed by Robert De Niro, orders his brother Joey to hit him in the face. After demurring as long as he can, Joey wraps his hand in a kitchen towel and socks Jake until Jake is left bleeding—and smiling for having endured the abuse. Joe Pesci's Joey acts on the idea that it is more important to respect his brother's wish, crazy as it seems to be, over the desire not to cause harm to his sibling. As unpleasant as it is to watch the scene, can we really conclude that Joey did the wrong thing?

The bottom line, however, is that when you feel pressured to choose one principle over another, you should do everything you can to step back for a moment to consider all of the possibilities open to you and how you can honor all five principles.

Taking the High Road When Others Don't

You are a person of conscience. You are a lifelong learner who is committed to being the best person you can be. You read books like this so that you can discover new ways of meeting the challenges you face every day.

You are also in the minority.

Or at least it seems that way. To paraphrase a George Carlin joke, have you ever noticed that on the highway everyone driving slower than you is an idiot, and everyone driving faster than you is a maniac? It seems that no matter how hard we try to do the right thing, our world is made up of people who take the low road at every opportunity, who behave dishonorably in their professional and personal relationships, and who do whatever is necessary to get what they want, regardless of how their actions affect others.

I'm not just talking about your ex-husband or former girlfriend, but about everyone in your orbit. "Why," you ask, "should I work so hard to do the right thing when so many people around me don't care about telling the truth, being fair, or adopting a loving attitude? What's in it for me?"

Why, indeed, you should you take the five Life Principles seriously at a time when our society seems to be at an all-time low with respect to ethical conduct? Each week we learn of yet another scandal in business, government, education, health care, or law enforcement. Our local papers regularly report indecent behavior, domestic violence, and sexual assault by someone in a position of authority. By the time we have reached "a certain age," bitterness about human nature sets in, and we are tempted to resign ourselves to cynicism and despair.

The most important reason that we should live by the Life Principles is that it is the right thing to do. Refraining from causing harm, making things better, respecting others, being fair, and acting with loving kindness brings out the best in us as it benefits and honors others. It helps us to become our richest, truest selves.

The fact that other people disregard the Life Principles is morally irrelevant to how we live our own lives. In golf, the primary rule is, "Keep your eye on the ball." Pros do not look around as they are about to swing; they maintain a laser-like focus on what they are doing. This is a good metaphor for living a happy and moral life. Ultimately the only control we have in life is over our own actions. We cannot write another person's script. We cannot make choices for others. All we can do is make the best choices we can, and the Life Principles provide the best framework for doing this. How other people—including our spouses, our adult children, our closest friends, and our coworkers— decide to live their lives is up to them.

Nevertheless, by taking the high road and not giving in to the temptation to think only about ourselves, we may very well serve as an example to others. Just as our parents, favorite teachers, close friends, and life partners inspire us to be the best we can be, so do our own noble actions light a candle for others. Recall James Stewart's character George Bailey in Frank Capra's *It's a Wonderful Life*. In the last third of the film, Bailey tells his guardian angel, Clarence, that he wishes he had never been born. Clarence grants Bailey his wish, and Bailey soon learns how much good he has done in life by seeing what would have happened in the community without him. Since he never saved his young brother's life, his brother wasn't around to save dozens of soldiers during the war. The town itself had degenerated into sleaziness overrun with rowdy nightclubs and prostitutes. Bailey, who had tried to leave his hometown for most of his adult life, realized that a life devoted to helping others made him beloved to all (except Lionel Barrymore's miser Mr. Potter, but you can't please everyone). The message of *It's a Wonderful Life* is that our loving actions can and do influence others in ways we aren't even aware of, and that message makes the film timeless.

Making the Life Principles Second Nature

In our hectic daily lives we don't have the time to pause and reflect upon the right course of action every time we are faced with a challenge. We wouldn't be able to get much done if every time we wonder, "What should I do?" we have to take a few minutes to consider how the Life Principles apply to the situation. How, then, can we incorporate the Life Principles into our lives in practical terms?

Aristotle notes in *Nicomachean Ethics* that just as we develop strong muscles by exercising them, so do we develop good character by performing good acts:

> The virtues...we acquire by first having put them into action, and the same is also true of

the arts. For the things which we have to learn before doing them we learn by doing: men become builders by building houses, and harpists by playing the harp. Similarly, we become just by performing just actions, self-controlled by exercising self-control, and courageous by performing acts of courage. [1]

As I stated in the introduction, I am not presenting anything new with these Life Principles, since we learned them when we were young. The purpose of this book is not to suggest a new way of living but rather to ask, "Do you remember these guidelines for how to live a good life?" Because we have already been taught them, the challenge is not to discover but to recover them, to recall their value, and to incorporate them into all that we do. Easier said than done?

Not really. The more frequently we take steps to avoid harming others, to make things better, to tell the truth and keep our promises, to be fair, and to act with loving kindness, the easier it is to do so. Getting out of a commitment by lying, to take one example of unethical conduct, is problematic not just because it dishonors a relationship but because it makes it easier for us to lie again. Just as we develop moral virtue by doing

[1] Aristotle, *Nicomachean Ethics*, trans. Martin Ostwald (Indianapolis: Liberal Arts Press, 1962), p. 34.

the right thing over and over again, so do we tarnish our souls by repeatedly taking the low road.

The ethics quiz at the beginning of this book presented three options to each scenario, but of course there are often four, five, or more choices before us in any given situation. More often than not, we know what we ought to do without having to analyze the implications of each Life Principle. The more frequently we do what is right rather than what is easy or convenient, the more inclined we are to take the high road another time.

LIVING BY THE PRINCIPLES: THE KEY TO A HAPPY LIFE

When I do good, I feel good; when I do bad, I feel bad,
and that is my religion.
—Abraham Lincoln

We have now examined many ways in which taking the high road is not only the right thing to do; it's good for us professionally and personally.

Still, one might meet the challenge to be ethical with skepticism, even cynicism. After all, the world is full of people who figuratively or literally get away with murder every day. Why, one might ask, should we bother incorporating the Life Principles into our day-to-day activities when it is so much easier to act selfishly? Why restrain hostile impulses when it feels better to give in to them? Why bother taking ethics seriously when so many others act unethically?

A powerful response to these questions comes from the Book of Deuteronomy in what Jews call the Torah and Christians call the Old Testament. These words are emblazoned on a shrine at the end of the United States Holocaust Memorial Museum, which presents the ultimate challenge in believing in the possibility that good will triumph over evil:

> *I have set before you life and death, blessing and curse; therefore choose life.*
> —**Deuteronomy 30:1–20** [1]

Ultimately, it is up to us to decide what kind of life we want to live. We can take the low road and think primarily or exclusively about our own needs and desires. We can steal when no one is looking, cheat whenever we are able, lie when it is convenient, or break promises when something better comes along. We can resolve conflict with force rather than persuasion, because in the short run it is possible to conquer with violence, but peaceable solutions take time and effort.

Or, we can reacquaint ourselves with the five Life Principles discussed in this book. If we are lucky, these principles were taught to us by loving parents and concerned teachers as we grew up. In every interaction we

---

[1] I am including this Biblical quotation to make a point about why we should take the high road in general. It is not intended to speak to the ethics of abortion.

can take a moment to think about how our words and deeds may affect other people, particularly the people we care the most about, and make our choices accordingly. We can realize that, yes, we are better off living a moral life. But we can also acknowledge that the main reason to do so is not for personal gain but simply because it is the right thing to do.

Whether you believe that the Life Principles are worth following because they form the core of your religious tradition, or because a society that is not founded in principles of respect and fairness is a society that is not worth living in, I hope that through the journey we've taken together you will want to reaffirm your commitment to avoiding harmful acts, making things better, respecting others, being fair, and incorporating love into your life. Life is a precious gift, and the Life Principles are the best way to express gratitude for that gift.

I'd like to close with an excerpt from President Abraham Lincoln's First Inaugural Address, which he gave on Monday, March 4, 1861:

> We are not enemies, but friends. We must not
> be enemies. Though passion may have strained,
> it must not break our bonds of affection. The

mystic chords of memory, stretching from every battlefield and patriot grave to every living heart and hearthstone all over this broad land, will yet swell the chorus of the Union, when again touched, as surely they will be, by the better angels of our nature.

It is time to let the better angels of our nature soar. Chances are they will come back to us and make our lives richer than we can possibly imagine.

YOUR ETHICS IQ REVISITED

The five Life Principles help to explain which choice is best in each scenario.

What would you do?

1. After leaving a grocery store, you notice a six-pack of soda sitting in an otherwise empty shopping cart in the parking lot. Would you:

   A) Leave the soda where it is.

   B) Take it and keep it.

   C) BRING IT BACK TO THE STORE.

"A" leaves open the possibility that someone else will take what doesn't belong to her. "B" is stealing. "C" allows the rightful owner to claim the soda, which he almost certainly will do after noticing that the item is missing. If you go a little bit out of your way, another person will get back what rightfully belongs to her. Perhaps someone else will do the same for you one day.
SCORE: A=2, B=1, C=3

2. A friend recently set you up on a blind date, which didn't go well. Your friend, who is extremely sensitive to criticism, asks you how it went. Would you:

A) Lie and say it went well.

B) TELL THE TRUTH.

C) Thank your friend for the set-up but be vague in your answer ("Well, we'll have to see; you never know about these things...").

Two ethical obligations appear to conflict here: Do no harm on one hand, and tell the truth on the other. It seems as though you cannot satisfy both. By asking you how the date went, however, your friend is telling you that he values the truth, whatever the consequences of learning the truth might be. Of course, it is one thing to tell the raw, unvarnished truth, and another to be honest but respectful of the date and your friend. By telling your friend the truth directly without undue harshness, you can honor your duty of veracity and spare your friend's feelings too. "B" is the right way to go.

SCORE: A=1, B=3, C=2

3. You are at a party and one of your friends has become intoxicated. As she prepares to leave the party and drive home, you tell her that she has

had too much to drink and that you will take her home. She rudely tells you to mind your own business. Would you:

A) Do as she says.

B) TAKE HER KEYS AWAY FROM HER AND ARRANGE FOR A WAY FOR HER TO GET HOME.

C) Call the police when she gets on the road and tell them that an inebriated person is on the loose.

As we saw in our discussion of Life Principle #1, it is not enough to "do no harm;" we must also take care to prevent harm to others, particularly harm that is reasonably foreseeable. You would violate this moral obligation if you chose "A." Choice "C" appears to fulfill your obligation to respect the right of your friend to make her own decision, but that right is not an absolute one, since none of us has the right to cause (or enable) injury to other people (unless you're a professional football player and it goes with the territory). Only "B" will prevent foreseeable harm to other people, even if it requires restricting your friend's freedom. By drinking too much, the woman in question has temporarily waived her right to do as she pleases, for she is not entitled to turn her car into a killing

machine. If the fallout is a loss of the friendship, you can justifiably say, "Goodbye, and good riddance!"
SCORE: A=1, B=3, C=2

4. You have just opened your own retail pharmacy. One of your competitors sells cigarettes, which bothers you, because you feel that health care professionals should do what they can to prevent harm to others. On the other hand, cigarette sales are lucrative, and it is getting harder and harder to make a decent living these days. Would you:

A) REFUSE TO SELL CIGARETTES.

B) Sell cigarettes but caution customers about the health risks of smoking.

C) Sell cigarettes but without the lecture.

Pharmacists in particular, and health care providers in general, have an ethical obligation to promote the health of their patients. Refusing to stock cigarettes hardly denies patients their right to purchase these items if they so desire, but selling them would compromise the primary mission of the pharmacist. As pharmacists across the country prove every day, it is possible to make a decent living in the field without compromising their professional standards. "A" is the best choice.
SCORE: A=3, B=2, C=1

5. Your friend asks you if you like the new dress she has just purchased. You think it looks horrible but don't want to hurt her feelings. Would you:

A) Tell her the truth.

B) **FIND SOMETHING ABOUT THE DRESS THAT YOU DO LIKE AND MENTION ONLY THAT ("RAYON IS SO EASY TO CARE FOR!").**

C) Use language that is accurate but deceptive ("It's incredible! I've never seen anything like it!").

Life Principle #3, Respect Others, seems to point in the direction of "A," since being honest is one of the ways that we apply this principle in everyday life. But is it safe to assume that our friend truly wants your opinion? That might be the case if the two of you were at a store trying out various outfits, but she has already bought the dress. Chances are what she wants is not your honest evaluation but validation that she made a good decision—according to her own tastes and preferences. In an episode of *I Love Lucy* in which Lucy promised to tell the truth for twenty-four hours, she chose "C" when asked for her opinion about some new furniture her friend had bought. "It looks like a dream," she responded, after having confided to Ethel that the room looked like a nightmare. This choice is technically correct but misleading. "B" allows you to avoid getting into the habit of being deceptive; after all, the more we deceive others, even for benevolent reasons, the easier it becomes to do so. "B" also validates your friend's choice and makes her feel good about the purchase without being dishonest. It is the best option of the three.

SCORE: A=1, B=3, C=2

6. You see an expensive article of clothing that you want but can't afford. Would you:

   A) SAVE YOUR MONEY AND BUY IT LATER.

   B) Buy it now, wear it once, and then return it.

   C) Sign up for the store's credit card or use one you have and get it now.

The fact that many people may choose "B" is not a justification for doing so. How would you feel if you bought a dress believing it to be new, only to find out later that someone had worn it? Our chances of being treated respectfully are better if we treat others with respect. "C" violates Life Principle #1, Do No Harm, since you burden yourself with a debt that may be difficult to pay off in a timely fashion. This principle applies to you (requiring that you refrain from harming yourself) as well as to the people with whom you come into contact. Also, if you make it a habit to charge items you can't pay for, you may wind up in bankruptcy, which violates Life Principle #4, Be Fair. After all, repaying our debts is one of the obligations this principle entails. "A" allows you to avoid violating these two principles. You'll be better off in the long run by choosing this option.

SCORE: A=3, B=1, C=2

7. You and your beloved are having dinner at a fancy restaurant to celebrate your anniversary. When the check arrives, you notice that the waiter forgot to include the expensive bottle of wine you had. Would you:

   A) Pay the bill without notifying the waiter of the omission but leave a larger tip than you had planned.

   B) Pay the bill as is and leave a normal tip.

   C) TELL THE WAITER ABOUT THE ERROR.

Your lucky accident will be at the waiter's expense, since he will have to pay for that bottle of wine out of his own pocket. How is that fair? You quaffed the wine, so you should pay for it. That is the only reasonable application of Life Principle #4 to this dilemma, which ultimately is a psychological rather than ethical one. It may feel tempting to keep the error to yourself, but there is no moral justification for doing so. Yes, the waiter made a mistake, but that doesn't mean it should cost him dearly. Pay the right amount, and the good night's rest you get tonight won't be entirely due to that lovely pinot noir you enjoyed.

SCORE: A=2, B=1, C=3

8. One evening while watching TV you discover that you are now receiving a premium cable channel that you have not ordered. After doing some research, you learn that the cable company has made a mistake; it is unwittingly providing the service without charging you for it. Would you:

A) Do nothing but enjoy the free service.

B) CONTACT THE CABLE COMPANY AND NOTIFY IT OF THE ERROR.

C) Wait a few weeks to see if you really watch the station that often; if not, call the cable company and have it removed.

Gomer Pyle's grandmother would consider "A" to be "ill-gotten gains," since you're getting something for nothing. "C" tries to have it both ways and fails on both accounts, since we do not have the moral authority to decide whether to keep the channel. That call is for the cable company to make, since it licenses the product to us. It is the company's property until we pay for it. By taking the high road and choosing "B," we may very well find that the cable company allows us to continue to receive the channel at no cost—a reward for being honest. But if it doesn't, it would be unfortunate but not unfair, since we are not owed freebies.

SCORE: A=1, B=3, C=2

9. While you are driving on the highway, a driver passes you and cuts you off as you're preparing to change lanes. You are startled and scared by his actions. Your children are in the back seat. Would you:

   A) Roll down your window and yell at the driver.

   B) Call the police on your cell phone while you're driving to notify them of the incident.

   C) STAY CALM AND DO WHAT IS NECESSARY TO PROTECT YOURSELF AND YOUR KIDS.

"A" highlights the difference between the questions, "What would you do?" and "What should you do?" The former is a psychological or sociological question; the latter is an ethical one. Many of us find it difficult on occasion to resist road rage. But the fact that many people express hostility in these situations doesn't justify doing so. Life Principle #1, Do No Harm, requires that we place the safety of our children above whatever desire we may have to pull a Dirty Harry in this situation. "B" appears to fulfill our duty to prevent harm to others and to bring the joker to justice, but using a cell phone while driving increases our chances of causing an accident. If we really want to take "Do No Harm" seriously, "C" is the way to go.

SCORE: A=I, B=2, C=3

10. A celebrity, once one of your favorites, was recently convicted of a serious offense and sentenced to prison. How do you feel about this?

   A) Glad that the person got what s/he deserved.

   B) SAD THAT SOMEONE YOU USED TO ADMIRE GAVE IN TO LESS-THAN-NOBLE IMPULSES.

   C) Numb.

It is not enough to do the right thing, or even to do the right thing for the right reason: Being the best we can be means feeling the right way, too. Imagine someone who took great glee in seeing a child get hurt. We would rightly say that such an individual has poor character. Ethics isn't just about appropriate conduct; it's also about developing the right emotional responses (and yes, it is possible to do so).

The German word "schadenfreude" refers to the common tendency to feel good about another's misfortune. But the fact that some people react this way in certain circumstances doesn't mean that it is a noble human trait. Such a disposition violates Life Principle #1, "Do No Harm," in two ways: By being mean-spirited, we are treating another person in an indecent way (even if he doesn't know it), and by giving in to our baser instincts, we are tarnishing our own souls. "A" is thus an inappropriate response. So is "C," because an occasion such as this calls for some kind of feeling.

A morally good person is disposed to react in the way suggested by "B." Even if the behavior of the celebrity in question was not merely unfortunate but truly unfair, it does not follow that we too should take the low road. Everyone wins in the long run when we appeal to the best part of ourselves both in how we act and how we react. (Of course, one should also be concerned about the victims of the celebrity's actions.)

The goal in becoming a decent human being ultimately means not only refusing to feel joy in another's sorrow (or to feel bad about another's success), but developing the right feelings so that we are moved to act appropriately.

SCORE: A=1, B=3, C=2

ACKNOWLEDGMENTS

In *The Tipping Point: How Little Things Can Make a Big Difference*, Malcolm Gladwell shows that one way that social trends get started and sustained is through the efforts of some folks who take the ideas developed by a theoretician and make those ideas broadly accessible. Reading Gladwell, I was prompted to think of author Thomas Moore, who acknowledged in his influential book *Care of the Soul* that the ideas contained therein were not original but derived from his mentor, psychoanalyst James Hillman. Moore took Hillman's powerful but difficult work, broke it down while being true to its spirit, and made it intelligible to lay readers.

With all due humility, this is what I have attempted to do here.

Even before attending Georgetown University's graduate program in philosophy with a concentration in bioethics, I was familiar with Tom L. Beauchamp and James F. Childress's pioneering work *Principles of Biomedical Ethics* (Oxford University Press, now in its fifth edition). While at Georgetown, I had the privilege of studying with Dr. Beauchamp, and after receiving my PhD and teaching at the Robert C. Byrd Health Sciences Center at West Virginia University, it occurred to me that the four principles Beauchamp and Childress present—nonmaleficence, beneficence, respect for autonomy, and justice—had the potential for application beyond the biomedical sciences. When I left academics to create my own ethics consultation company, I decided to broaden the scope of my teaching to include law, business, education, and community service as well as medicine, dentistry, pharmacy, nursing, and social work. I found that the framework discussed in *Principles of Biomedical Ethics* served as a useful tool for helping members of these diverse groups think through ethical problems at work and beyond. I decided to use the more plaintive terms, "do no harm," "makes things better," "respect others," and "be fair," to refer to the Beauchamp/Childress quartet of principles, and I have added a fifth one, "be loving," for reasons I discuss in the corresponding chapter. These five ideas I am calling "Life Principles," because following them is not just the right thing to do but the best way to enrich our lives. Beauchamp and Childress do discuss the ethics of care in their book, and "be loving" might be considered a cornerstone of that ethical system, so in no way do I take credit for originating any of the ideas contained herein. All I have tried to do is to take this towering, scholarly work and present it to readers beyond the academic world.

To fulfill this goal, I was fortunate to have a wonderful literary agent, June Clark of the Peter Rubie Literary Agency, on my team. Both June and Peter helped me enormously in preparing the book proposal, and June was tireless in her efforts to secure the right publisher for the book. With Emmis Books we found a most hospitable home. Richard Hunt, Jack Heffron, and Jessica Yerega of Emmis have been a joy to work with, and they have helped me to make this the best possible work it can be. Thank you all.

ABOUT THE AUTHOR

Bruce Weinstein, PhD, is the professional ethicist known as The Ethics Guy™. He appears weekly on CNN for "Ask the Ethics Guy," a question-and-answer segment modeled after his Knight Ridder/Tribune syndicated column of the same name. His interactive talks to businesses, schools, and nonprofit organizations across the country show how living an ethical life makes us happier, healthier, and more prosperous.

Dr. Weinstein is the author or editor of four previous books and the author of more than twenty articles on ethics. His writings have appeared in, or he has been featured in, the *New York Times*, the *Los Angeles Times*, the *Christian Science Monitor*, the *New York Observer*, *Time*, *Investor's Business Daily*, the *Journal of the American Medical Association*, the *New England Journal of Medicine*, *Family Circle*, *Woman's World*, *Men's Fitness*, and *American Way*, the magazine of American Airlines.

In addition to his CNN duties, Dr. Weinstein has appeared as an ethics analyst on ABC TV's *Good Morning America*, NBC TV's *Early Today*, the Fox News Channel's *O'Reilly Factor*, *MSNBC Live*, CNBC's *Capital Report*, Bloomberg Television's *Personal Finance*, Fox TV's *Good Day New York*, and other programs.

He received a bachelor's degree in philosophy from Swarthmore College, a doctorate in philosophy and bioethics from Georgetown University, and a certificate in film production from New York University.

Dr. Weinstein is also an independent filmmaker and is producing a documentary about an ex-mobster who is devoting the remainder of his life to discouraging young people from becoming criminals. Dr. Weinstein was invited to participate in the Sundance Institute's Independent Producers Conference on behalf of this work-in-progress.

Dr. Weinstein is a W.K. Kellogg National Fellow and lives in New York.

To contact him, please visit www.TheEthicsGuy.com or e-mail Bruce@TheEthicsGuy.com.